What people are saying about …

WALKING TO
JERUSALEM

"Finding and walking into your God-ordained purpose is critical to living a fulfilling and purpose-filled life. In his new book, *Walking to Jerusalem*, Chris Hill shows us how to do just that. By unlocking his own life journey and the life of King David, Chris shows us how to find our own path to our own Jerusalem."

Christine Caine, founder of The A21 Campaign

"The events of David's life informed his future, and these same insights can help you find and fulfill your own purpose. *Walking to Jerusalem* is about using whatever situation you're in to discover your destiny and fulfill it God's way."

Steven Furtick, pastor of Elevation Church
and *New York Times* bestselling author

"Finding your purpose is a journey with many ebbs and flows. My friend Pastor Chris Hill uses the life of David to reveal how your journey shapes your future. *Walking to Jerusalem* will inspire and encourage you to go after your purpose with greater passion."

John Bevere, author, minister, and
founder of Messenger International

"Pastor Chris Hill is a once-in-a-generation leader and a brilliant communicator with a passion for life and love for the Word of God. His desire to see people journey through life with an overcoming spirit and an understanding of the value and calling that God places upon them will leave a lasting impact. His personal experience and revelations from the highs and lows of life will resonate with you and prove valuable and applicable to your own spiritual journey."

Brian Houston, founder and global senior pastor of Hillsong Church, and international bestselling author of *LIVE LOVE LEAD*

"Chris Hill's life and ministry have influenced me for a long time. He loves his wife, leads his family, and builds God's church. His sermons have helped so many, including the many preachers like me who humbly glean from them (also known as outright theft). What I love about this book is how Chris finds a link that leads to Jesus in everything. As David walked through so many cities and seasons, beautifully laid out in this book, so will we all! Chris helps us understand that God has a purpose even when we can't yet see it, feel it, or grasp it. This book could be described as a road map, and it will lead people closer to God."

Carl Lentz, lead pastor of Hillsong NYC

"In *Walking to Jerusalem* Pastor Chris Hill empowers us with the transformative knowledge that the purpose of God is always greater than the brokenness of man. Extrapolating life lessons from the life of King David, Chris Hill, one of the most anointed and gifted leaders in the kingdom today, takes us on a journey that reconciles process with progress, obedience with overflow, and repentance with redemption. This walk will change your life!"

Rev. Dr. Samuel Rodriguez, president of NHCLC/CONELA Hispanic Evangelical Association, latinoevangelicals.com

"In *Walking to Jerusalem* Dr. Chris Hill will take you on a journey using the life of David. In each and every city something is discovered in David's life that will help you discover something in your life. This book is a must-read for all those on the journey to discovering their God-given destiny."

Benny Perez, lead pastor of The Church LV

"I love the message that Chris Hill brings in *Walking to Jerusalem*. Such powerful lessons can be learned from the life of David that speak so clearly to us no matter what stage of the journey we are in. Many people get discouraged in life and miss what God has for them simply because they don't understand the process God is using to develop them. This book will inspire you to embrace that process and give you vision for what God is doing in your life so you can have a lasting impact."

Banning Liebscher, founder and pastor of Jesus Culture

"Dr. Chris Hill's book *Walking to Jerusalem* is a powerful book full of amazing biblical and practical revelation. Dr. Hill is one of the world's great orators, thinkers, and leaders. His book will create a life-changing moment in your life. I thoroughly recommend *Walking to Jerusalem*. It's a must-read!"

Russell Evans, founder, director, and
senior pastor of Planetshakers Church

"Pastor Chris Hill's new book, *Walking to Jerusalem*, is a powerful must-read for those who are searching for their God-given purpose. By taking you through King David's amazing journey, Pastor Hill provides a deep perspective on God's great plan for your life. This book is a bold and daring challenge to trust God completely and experience Him in a new way."

Pastor Wilfredo "Choco" De Jesús,
senior pastor of New Life Covenant Church
in Chicago, *Time* magazine's 100 Most
Influential People in the World 2013, and
author of *Amazing Faith* and *In the Gap*

"Over twenty years ago I was sitting around a table of young preachers and first heard Pastor Chris Hill teach on the twelve cities of David. The revelation I received on that day changed the entire course of my life! In *Walking to Jerusalem* he has fused the journey of David, the shepherd boy who was transformed through pain and problems into a powerful king, together with his own transparent story of one who survived abandonment and homelessness as a child and became a successful businessman and international evangelist. In this book Chris Hill will walk with you through your 'cities' and help you discover the possibilities that wait for you in your Jerusalem."

Dr. Craig W. McMullen, senior associate
pastor of The Potter's House of Denver

"Often people see the success of our glory but never understand the challenges of our story. This is a masterful and insightful look into young David's journey to King David. My friend Pastor Chris Hill has given us a transparent look into his own challenges and successes and with courage has written a guide to help us all achieve our God-given destiny. This is a must-read for those needing clarity along the way to greatness."

Bishop Joseph Warren Walker III, senior
pastor of Mt. Zion Baptist Church in
Nashville and presiding bishop of Full Gospel
Baptist Church Fellowship International

"Dr. Hill's book *Walking to Jerusalem* is an amazing journey from what men do to what God can do. Dr. Hill shows all of us how to get from our rags to our royalty, from our fields to our palaces, and from our struggles to God's destiny. You will be encouraged, empowered, and lifted to new heights as you read. You'll learn the spiritual and practical truths that will change your future. You will love the inspiration and information that will influence your life as much as it did mine."

Casey Treat, senior pastor of the
Christian Faith Center in Seattle

"For nearly thirty years since I first heard Myles Munroe speak about purpose, I've been a student of the subject. From Bruce Wilkinson's *The Dream Giver* to Rick Warren's *The Purpose Driven Life*, God's intentionality over our lives has inspired and motivated me to help others fulfill their purpose through education and advocacy. I have never, however, read such an inspirational and compelling treatment of this subject as *Walking to Jerusalem* by Pastor Chris Hill. With a divinely masterful use of King David's cities as metaphors, interspersed with stories of his own journey, Pastor Chris authentically unveils the truth that God's path from kid to king involves a process of refinement and growth, failures and faith, and challenges to victory. I encourage everyone seeking God's purpose to walk to Jerusalem."

Karl W. Reid, EdD, executive director of
National Society of Black Engineers

"There are individuals in each generation who create such impact they cannot be ignored, dismissed, or forgotten. David the son of Jesse from the town of Bethlehem was indeed such a figure. I know you will find this latest work of my dear friend Chris Hill to be an experience that challenges you to believe that no matter the giants you face, you have been chosen to wear the crown of a conqueror. As you look at the life of David, who served his generation, you will come to realize that the book you hold was written by a man of God who has been given a voice that is shaping his. In the years I have known Chris, he has proven himself to be faithful to encourage, to lead with a servant's heart, to be loyal in his friendships, and above all else to preach the Word. I am honored to recommend *Walking to Jerusalem* to you."

Matthew Hagee, executive pastor of
Cornerstone Church in San Antonio

"Few leaders in ministry walk with the kind of 'God confidence' exhibited by Pastor Chris Hill. Every time I hear him speak, I'm encouraged to trust God more. After reading *Walking to Jerusalem*, I understand even more why Pastor Hill communicates with such a sure voice. He has walked through—and to—many different places, each providing a life and leadership lesson that he carries today. This compelling book combines the journeys of King David, from boyhood to manhood, with the practical experiences of Pastor Hill, leaving the reader with greater understanding and boldness to follow Christ, wherever He may lead. I wholeheartedly recommend *Walking to Jerusalem*—it's a fantastic companion through the sometimes confusing, always challenging, journey of life."

Steve Kelly, senior pastor of Wave
Church in Virginia Beach

"I love this new book by Chris Hill. It speaks of the process of spiritual growth and discovering our purpose as we are a chosen people. As you read this book, you will learn how to walk with Jesus and discern His design for your life, as it is determined by your willingness to trust and put your faith in him."

Chris Durso, Christ Tabernacle/ MISFIT NYC

WALKING *to* JERUSALEM

DISCOVERING YOUR DIVINE LIFE PURPOSE

CHRIS HILL

David ⓒ Cook®

transforming lives together

WALKING TO JERUSALEM
Published by David C Cook
4050 Lee Vance View
Colorado Springs, CO 80918 U.S.A.

David C Cook Distribution Canada
55 Woodslee Avenue, Paris, Ontario, Canada N3L 3E5

David C Cook U.K., Kingsway Communications
Eastbourne, East Sussex BN23 6NT, England

The graphic circle C logo is a registered trademark of David C Cook.

LCCN 2016931981
ISBN 978-1-4347-1014-7
eISBN 978-1-4347-1020-8

Published in association with the literary agency
of The Fedd Agency, Inc., Austin, TX

The Team: Tim Peterson, Nick Lee, Cara Iverson, Tiffany Thomas, Susan Murdock
Cover Design: Amy Konyndyk
Cover Photo: Don Jones Photography
Background Images: Getty Images and iStockphoto

Printed in the United States of America
First Edition 2016

1 2 3 4 5 6 7 8 9 10

030716

For
Christopher Hill Jr. and Jonathon Hill

CONTENTS

Foreword

I vividly remember walking into the reception held after a commemorative service for the fallen victims of the 2012 movie theater assault in Aurora, Colorado. In the room were city leaders gathered from near and far, sharing stories of a man and his visionary approach to leadership. This young pastor had given comfort to the families and friends of those tragically taken from us in the senseless shooting that ended many lives and broke many hearts. I was astounded by how his leadership brought together a fragmented, shocked, and devastated city. He clearly was a man of considerable tenacity and character. Could this truly be the boy who had walked into my office many years before, nervous and uneasy? How was it possible that the man who had created such a buzz in this city was the same young man who had helped redefine youth ministry in my church only a few short years before?

Let me explain my nostalgia …

The year was 1997 and it was an unforgettable moment in my life. I was a pastor newly arrived to the Dallas–Fort Worth metroplex, fresh from the hills of West Virginia. I couldn't imagine how I had come to be in such a robust, thriving city. I had founded a church that in no way resembled the church I grew up in, or the

15

ones I had pastored before. You can imagine the care I exercised in deciding who would compose the team of leaders who stood beside me as I pioneered this path. The team I chose would not only be with me but also with the community I served and the church I pastored.

After only the first year, I had been bombarded with bombastic and opportunistic ploys leading to wrong choices that only a new pastor can make. During those first twelve months, I learned the hard way to be extremely careful about whom I chose to make up my core team. I found myself in need of a youth pastor, as my former one had tried to split my church while it was in its embryonic stages. I needed someone gifted, articulate, and spiritually grounded, yet creative enough to capture the imagination of a youth department that was bruised and scattered from my last selection.

I had to be careful to avoid the type of aspirational servant who moves from place to place, trying to exploit the goodwill and hard work of others, cannibalizing their fruitful labor, and catapulting from that stage into their own agenda. As my mother would say, "A burned child dreads fire!" I had been burned; I needed to be certain I had the man for the job!

After a long search, I was scheduled to meet a young man from Boston whose résumé lauded both experience and intellect. If his résumé was any indication, it seemed as if he might be a fit for our church.

The interview hadn't gone on long before I realized this man was the perfect choice and that we were destined to intersect for kingdom purposes. My heart beat fast with excitement because I could sense that he possessed the power, theological prowess, and spiritual potential to accomplish the assignment. I was excited.

Dr. Chris E. Hill was slight of stature but robust in power, demonstrating a strong and profound grasp of the components necessary to build a progressive ministry to youth. I knew that the ground he needed to plow would be tough and unrelenting. The landscape was riddled with casualties associated with the sociological conundrum that exists in inner-city ministry. And though he was from the pristine Ivy League environment of Boston, he was indeed adroit enough to forge the divide and reach the underserved, while still being relevant to the more savored areas of our society. Little did I know that I was the one "on assignment" to tend the garden and provide the fertile ground for far more than a youth pastor. I had interviewed and then hired the man who would become a giant slayer for the next generation.

Chris Hill was a young pastor who would go on to revolutionize our ministry to an urban community in the southern sector of Dallas. But even more, he would grow to become an international voice, traveling the globe and impacting all cultures and communities. He walked with a lion's share of influence and a heart filled with empathy for a world fallen into utter depravity. I was to tend the fields and watch him gather stones that later would be hurled toward the skull of a Goliath that had devoured so many of his predecessors.

I prayed for him as a young man, and now I cheer him on: my youth pastor has become a pastor of pastors, a confidant to elected officials, and a change agent for corporate leaders. Chris is a man who has cleared the brush, found the path, and stepped from obscurity into the harsh and brilliant light of twenty-first-century leadership.

Chris and his lovely wife, Joy, who is a gifted and vibrant asset in her own right, have become world ambassadors for Jesus Christ.

His command of Scripture, though massive, doesn't deter from the depth of his understanding of cultures, calibration, and conquering kingdom coordinates. These attributes are wired into Chris's "control tower" and have assisted in his liftoff into a destiny that has influenced—and will continue to influence—the world and will empower the generation for whom he is clearly heir apparent!

Today he pastors the legendary Potter's House of Denver. Here from a postured post of influence, his voice defines the ethics and theological relevance that have helped guide countless others into their destinies, both secular and sacred. I am, therefore, not at all surprised that *Walk to Jerusalem: Discovering Your Divine Life Purpose* has the accreditation of a journey I have observed and influenced. Chris clearly has gathered wisdom that is bookworthy. Each page chronicles for us a theological dissertation accentuated by personal experience, designed so the reader will see the Davidic text from which he draws metaphorical content. This journey will guide the reader to find and achieve his or her purpose.

David was chosen against all odds to reign and rule from a background of debris—one that seemed counterintuitive to his ultimate destiny. He was a kid whose background was an oxymoron for his future. In the way one watches a caterpillar morph into a butterfly, I see both David and Chris detangle themselves from the cocoon of yesterday and emerge into the cacophony of a world filled with pestilence and problems, leading us from darkness to the brilliance of enlightenment.

I have watched as the boy who once sat at my desk with uncertainty has not only grown into an excellent father but also has come to church to serve as a son. I've been fascinated as Chris, with vigilance and perseverance, has gathered his own shredded childhood and transformed its perilous beginnings into a mosaic of possibility. In so doing, he has robbed all spectators of the plausibility of blaming the past for current or future underachievement. Instead, he has demanded that we throw our rocks toward every obstacle that could or would deter us from evolving into our purpose.

Chris's wisdom, directions, and observations should be read only by those who sense that beneath the rubble of obstacles and adversities in their own lives lies a champion waiting—no, longing—to emerge. With one hand Chris constructs a solid argument for building in spite of barriers, and with the other he takes a stirring and often compassionate look at the maladies and miracles littering the road to a destiny that defies description. If adhered to, his thoughts may lessen the learning curve when it comes to the proverbial question, *What's next?*

If you have ever thought the odds were against you, you must read this book. If you have felt destiny was playing a rousing game of hide-and-seek, you must read this missive. For this message is a guided missile that will assist you in securing direction and a clear definition of purpose, power, and passion, destroying all excuses that would be barriers and deterrents along the way.

Later in his life, I laid my hands on Chris Hill as the first senior pastor of The Potter's House of Denver, which I had the confidence to consecrate into a church that, while separate, is akin to the one where he stood in my shadow and watched me build during the previous decade. Now my former youth pastor has become a man. More than that, he is the visionary for The Potter's House of Denver. His rapid growth has led to the record-setting gathering of thousands of souls aligned toward his vision there. The vast and varied giftings of this leader have garnered a wide array of upwardly mobile thought leaders and influencers with credentials even his enemies and critics cannot deny.

It is indeed an honor and a deep pleasure to welcome Dr. Hill's readers to join this journey into the relentless pursuit of purpose! *Walking to Jerusalem*, within the title itself, undermines the common idea that a journey is a speeding car chase; it is not. Nor is a journey a sprint. Instead, a God-driven journey is a walk, and sometimes a crawl—but it always consistently moves forward to an expected end. As with any journey that causes us to embark on a new mission to a foreign place, a guide is always helpful.

Perhaps you are grappling with the notion of an adventurous life—a transition from the mediocre and mundane to the mighty and manicured terrain of a grounded truth about what is possible to the person who believes. If so, this book is for you.

Therefore, I'm proud to present the writings, thoughts, and directives of a young man whose track record is indisputable. The next several hundred pages will help readers escape what is, and discover what is possible for those who believe. Ladies and gentlemen, brothers and sisters, prepare your hearts and minds for the journey within and without that will help you escape the gravitational pull of normalcy and land you safely into God's best will and plan for your life!

Bishop T. D. Jakes Sr.
The Potter's House of Dallas

ACKNOWLEDGMENTS

I want to thank so many people for helping me on this brave new journey:

First, to my wonderful wife, Joy, for listening to me as I talked out each chapter long into the night. My two strong sons, Chris and Jon, for being the greatest inspiration for sharing my own story. To my mother and my late father, who are the cowriters of my identity and who cheered for me before anyone even knew my name.

My literary agent, Esther Fedorkevich, for forcing me to get out of the boat and to Cara Highsmith for holding my hand as I walked across the waves. To my publisher, David C Cook, for seeing my heart to minister to people and for being willing to let me borrow their megaphone to share it with the world.

To my pastors, Bishop T. D. Jakes and Mrs. Serita Jakes, for mentoring me into my destiny, one step at a time. And to my faithful church family and staff at The Potter's House of Denver for allowing God to make these chapters come to life as I shared them first with you from our pulpit in the mountains.

To all the men and women who have coached me, prayed for me, trained me, encouraged me, supported me, challenged me, and mentored me, I am who I am becoming because you cared.

And last, to all my brothers and sisters in the ministry, in business, in academia, and in the media who have opened their hearts and their doors for me to share this word across the entire world.

Introduction

Ye are a chosen generation, a royal priesthood, an holy nation,
a peculiar people; that ye should shew forth the praises of him
who hath called you out of darkness into his marvellous light.

1 Peter 2:9

When I was a kid growing up in church, our congregation sang a song based on this scripture from 1 Peter. I was raised in an African American church, so although other churches sang this song one way, we sang it with our own style. We sang it fast and vigorously, with the entire congregation clapping and swaying. The robe-clad worship leader, microphone in hand, would instruct us to sing it just "one more time"—which would invariably turn into ten more times. We sang until the musicians would increase the tempo and the whole church would break into dance.

Inspiring as the experience was, I questioned the words of that song, because I didn't yet know they were taken from Scripture. The bold declarations challenged me. These words were not about Jesus, as were most of the songs we sang. These words were not even being sung *to* Jesus. These words we sang so boldly were about *us*.

When I investigated further and discovered that these words were from the Bible, I was dumbfounded. The Holy Spirit inspired the apostle to describe the people of the New Testament church in such a grandiose way that it blew my mind. Saint Peter used words such as *chosen*, *holy*, and *royal*, so I began to examine their meaning slowly, not in the fast pace of our church. I considered them prayerfully and methodically, trying hard to understand.

I can easily wrap my mind around the word *chosen* because I am thankful that Jesus chose me. This word presupposes that I did not *earn* my position or status. Outside the realm of my will and ability, God extended His grace toward me and—*whamo!*—I was chosen.

Being chosen makes me feel grateful and happy, like a kid picked first for a playground game of basketball. Captain Jesus chose me for His team, even though He already knows I can't play well. Such grace is truly amazing, and I understand why our congregation sang that part of the song with such joy.

When I got to the word *holy*, however, things started to become more complicated. Being holy has different connotations to different people. Even mainstream Christian denominations and orthodox religious organizations interpret that word in myriad ways. Wars have been fought over what was "holy." Churches have split and denominations have divided over what was considered holy. Confused, I walked into my pastor's study, went right up to his bookshelf, and pulled out one of his dusty old Greek books. I looked up the word *holy* and saw that it simply means "set apart for sacred use."

Once you strip the word of the differing theological labels and deal with it at face value, it becomes fairly easy to grasp. God has set us apart to be used by Him to change our world. I will not debate what makes or keeps someone holy. That debate has raged since long before I was born and will persist long after I am gone. But we can all understand that to be holy is to be set apart, to be used by God in the world.

At my church in Denver, we have special silver trays used to serve Communion the first Sunday of the month. These trays happen to be the right dimensions for serving pizza to the youth on Friday nights, but the elders would probably fire the brazen youth pastor for doing that, because these trays are considered holy. The trays have been chosen—set apart—for the sole purpose of serving Communion. And we, the New Testament church, were sovereignly selected (chosen) by the grace of God and set apart (holy) to be used by Him in the world.

With this in mind, I felt I was tracking really well with Saint Peter until I got to the word *royal*. I knew most of the people in my little church, and they were definitely not royalty. Most were just honest, hardworking people. Some were, to my mind, really pious and praying people, but nobody singing that song was royal, myself included. No one owned a castle or wore a crown. We couldn't be royal, as we all lived in the 'hood.

I felt that St. Peter either was stretching it a bit with that word or he had never visited my home church. This idea of royalty threw me, so I went back to my pastor's Greek books to look up the word. Come to find out, the Greek word for *royal* didn't have any variations or other meanings; it just meant "royal."

This insight set me on a path of discovery. I wanted to fully understand how God could possibly see us as royal. I am not one to break up Scripture and discard parts that don't make sense, so how could I accept the other words describing the New Testament church but dismiss the third word? I couldn't. If we were chosen and holy, then we also had to be royal, even if I could not understand how.

Stuck on the concept of royalty I was familiar with—kings and queens sitting on thrones, wearing crowns and tiaras—I saw none of this in the faithful people in the pews. But that could not negate the truth of the Word of God, so I began to pray for guidance. Then I began to study the Scriptures. I wanted to understand this path to royalty God intended for believers. Was this a heaven-bound promise or an earthly reality? Was this just pie in the sky, or could a person really reign on earth? And what did it mean to reign on earth anyway?

I wrestled with these questions until, in prayer, I realized that in the biblical context, *ruling* people was akin to *serving* people. Despotic domination of others is not the intent of Scripture. When God says "royal" in His kingdom, He is talking about the realm of service where He has placed each of us. Royalty is for the benefit of others.

As I continued to pray on this idea, the Holy Spirit began to lead me into a deep study of the life of David. During this study, I assembled the puzzle pieces of his life, recognizing a pattern that emerged. David's life began to unlock for me the path that an ordinary person could walk to become royal.

By studying David's life, I discovered that royalty does not always start on thrones. God calls you *royal* at the very moment you discover His divine purpose for your life. Discovering your own life purpose is critical to your promotion as a believer because you cannot reign if you have no clue where your kingdom is. Prince Charles is slated to be the king of England one day. In America, we celebrate and salute him, but he will never be our sovereign. America is no longer part of his kingdom, and no matter how many crowns he dons, he will never be our king. Charles can rule only in the territory where he has been given dominion.

Likewise, we cannot rule in an area where God has not already given us dominion. We become servant-leaders in the areas He has providentially appointed us. Our leadership is not to serve ourselves solely but also to benefit those around us. Divine life purpose helps us discern the parameters of our calling and understand how to maximize our personal impact.

Knowing your divine life purpose is the *initiation*, not the *culmination*, of this royal dimension in your life. David's first anointing was much earlier than his actual crowning. So although these two events—anointing and crowning—were connected, they were separated by a number of key events in his life. I saw that God strategically walked David through distinct places, with each "city" engineered to elicit a specific level of character development that would prepare him to rule. Journeying through each new place added a deeper dimension to his life.

I began to see startling parallels between David's progress toward his calling and my own life story. Insight and strength began to pour out of David's story and into my own life as if the biblical pages had come alive for me. I delved into these parallels, pulling from more than twenty years of pastoring people and mentoring leaders. I recognized many similarities that related directly to the people to whom I was ministering. I saw a pattern in the details of David's long walk to the throne and a progression that could be applied to any believer's life. God first *purposes* us and then *prepares* us.

As I began to share this new understanding, my ministry began to change. I preached and taught this progression as the "Cities of David," and requests for speaking appearances exploded. Leaders called for me from across the nation and around the world because this message resonated with their desire to discover and fulfill their own divine life purpose.

In my speaking, I revealed the darkest moments of my life and shared the losses that crystallized my own calling. Because my transparency coincided with a step-by-step progression of David in the Scriptures, the message became potent. Leaders began to realize they were holy, chosen, and royal despite where they started. They left my sessions encouraged and empowered, appreciating what they had been through and were going through but also anticipating what God still had in store. The phones in my office rang off the hook, and my website was flooded with more invitations than I could possibly fulfill. I was already speaking 250 times in one calendar year. It was then that I realized I needed to write a book on this subject.

It became clear this was an important message that I needed to share in the personal, in-depth way that only a book can. Speaking is a powerful tool, and I have been blessed to speak to millions of people over the last twenty years, but a book has the power to mentor and instruct at a much deeper level. I pray that it serves as a tool to guide you into your purpose for many years to come.

By unwrapping the biblical story of David, we will unwrap *you*. In this book, I will be transparent with you—sharing my own "cities" and revealing my own pains and challenges—so that by both real-life example and biblical precept, you can discover your own life purpose. This book is designed to help you find it if you don't know it or refine it if you already know the direction you are heading.

Once you know the realm God has destined you to rule—or rather, serve—so many things begin to fall into place. You will gain a retrospective understanding of your own life. You will fully understand what God was teaching you from the "cities" you have already walked through, you will become attuned to the cities He has you walking in currently, and you will be equipped for the ones He has you walking toward.

Finding your own life purpose is just the initial step. This book is designed to help you walk gracefully through the other "cities" until you have truly realized your life goal. David's life provides the perfect backdrop for this discussion, because in it we see God literally take him from being a kid to being a king—from rags to royalty. I pray that as you read this book, the same miracle will unfold in your life.

1

BETHLEHEM

The City of Beginnings

The Bethlehem of David's day was a town nestled in the hill country of Judah, where barley and wheat fields and peaceful pastureland covered the quiet countryside. Leading to many of the trade routes of Palestine, this small settlement sat less than six miles from the historic city of Jerusalem, which, at the time of David's birth, was a walled citadel occupied by the Canaanites.

Just north of Bethlehem is where in joy and sadness Jacob buried his bride Rachel and embraced her second son, Benjamin. In the valley just to the east are the fields where Ruth met Boaz, and from their union came Obed. From this storied family, the boy David emerged without fanfare or celebration. His birth was not heralded by angels or announced by bearded prophets. He was born of an unknown woman into what we would consider to be just another large family in Israel. Like Benjamin, the son of Jacob, David was the last son born into the household, but his mother was not a vaunted matriarch in Israel. Her identity is uncertain.

Because David rose to the pinnacle of power and the women of Israel sang songs about him in the streets, it is highly unusual that his mother's name would not even be recorded. We would expect a clear record of her in the biblical account, yet she is lost to history. This causes some scholars to speculate that perhaps his mother was not his father's (Jesse's) first wife and perhaps not even his wife at all. This son who was named David, meaning "beloved," could have been a love child brought into the home of his father, born under a cloud of shame that was later overlooked by the historians, evaporated in the bright light of his fame.

Later we read that the prophet Samuel came to the house of Jesse and asked to see all his sons. David was left out in the pasture to look after the sheep while all his older brothers were called in to dine with the seer. When Samuel insisted, David finally came into the house, where he was viewed and then anointed by the prophet (1 Sam. 16).

The family dynamic is again called into question when, in the next chapter, we see how David's eldest brother treated him with unveiled disdain: "Eliab his oldest brother heard when he spoke to the men; and Eliab's anger was aroused against David, and he said, 'Why did you come down here? And with whom have you left those few sheep in the wilderness? I know your pride and the insolence of your heart, for you have come down to see the battle.' And David said, 'What have I done now? Is there not a cause?'" (17:28–29 NKJV).

We also have David's own statements in Scripture, such as, "I was brought forth in iniquity, and in sin my mother conceived me" (Ps. 51:5 NKJV). We cannot say with certainty that this psalm is literal, but it is clear in his statement that David viewed his own birth in a humble way. In the vulnerability of his song to the Lord, we see the openness of his heart and are left to ponder the details of his birth. This psalm was composed *after* he himself fathered a child out of wedlock with a married woman, compounding the questions we have about the conditions that formed his familial mind-set.

The biblical record leaves us with many questions about this man we think we know so well. But reading David's life story, we see that in the end he was crowned and lauded as a great king throughout history, which tells us that it really doesn't matter where we begin; what matters is how we finish. We should be encouraged that the twists and turns of our own lives—including our failures—will not stop God from perfecting His purpose in us.

The questions that arise about David's life echo the questions I encounter when huddled with people in prayer circles. They are the questions I have heard so many ask of God for the last twenty-five years of my ministry: Where did I come from? Where am I going? These are the questions I wrestled with in my own soul and are probably why I was so drawn to study the life of David. The nature of his beginnings in Bethlehem are so similar to my own beginnings. By seeking to understand the development of David and his progression into finding and fulfilling his purpose, I slowly found my own.

WE ALL LIVE IN SMALL TOWNS

I was born and raised in a big city, but in a section that was similar to a small town. Four major roads in my community— Washington Street, Dorchester Avenue, Warren Street, and

Blue Hill Avenue—formed the axis of my entire world and defined the parameters of my existence. Boston is a city of neighborhoods, each one a separate small world unto itself built around class and ethnic affinity. The people my age all graduated from the same high school, just a few blocks from the elementary schools where we learned to play basketball. We grew up going to the same corner stores and bodegas, where the shop owners knew us by name and favorite snack. Generations of families made up the faithful members of the same churches and social clubs. You might have worked downtown, but you shopped, ate, dated, married, and worshipped in your neighborhood.

I find this scenario is true of most people. Their lives are lived not in cities but in the blocks that compose them. They might claim to be from a big city, but the parameters of their lives are contained in just the few miles that surround their homes. We all essentially live in small towns. The ideas of rural and urban living are illusory on a relational level: we all live in the small towns of the people we know and relate to directly.

The human heart is limited in how many people it can connect to, and no level of urban development can change that fact. We tend to carve out our piece of the city and call it our own, even if the population numbers in the millions. We cannot know them all. We mentally reduce our worlds to small, manageable "Bethlehems" populated by familiarity, predictability, and family. Being raised with this small-town mind-set affects how we perceive our lives. The way we view our futures can be limited and limiting when seen solely through the eyes of where we were born.

As a boy, I could not imagine I would ever live anywhere but Roxbury. I knew how to find my school, my park, and my church on Dudley Street. My family members lived just a few blocks away, all of them living in similar green triple-decker walk-ups and cooking up the familiar southern foods of their Georgia roots.

I knew where the bully gangs were and what streets to avoid. I knew the names of the addicts who sat sentry on the stairs of our tenement and the old ladies who seemed to live in the windows. I knew the location of the hospital where I was born and the library where I learned to read and began to dream. I never thought I would leave my small town. Thank God, I was wrong.

WE ALL HAVE TO FIND OUR PLACE AND PURPOSE

The dreams that began there in my small community may not have been big enough to take me beyond the city limits, but they were the seeds of purpose God planted in me. The first step to fulfilling your own purpose is to allow God to challenge the parameters of your own perception—to give the Creator permission to push you to imagine a world outside of your understanding. Perhaps you will never physically venture beyond the borders of your small town, but your mind is far too powerful to be bound to any particular zip code, neighborhood, block, or street. Once you give God permission to enlarge your vision, you can begin to dream.

Many people die having never lived. The graveyards are rich with the potential of great people who died with a small-town mentality and never released all they had inside. I was headed that way. I was Roxbury born and Roxbury bred and believed when I died I would be Roxbury dead, just as all the other children I grew up with. Similarly, I don't believe that David dreamed beyond the pastures of Bethlehem to the royal palaces he would rule one day.

I thought I might be a police officer like my father; no other idea or image ever came into my mind. I didn't know of anyone who had left our community to become a world evangelist. No one in my neighborhood had written books, traveled, or spoken to large groups. I had never even seen a black evangelist on television or heard one on the radio. I knew that Rev. Dr. Martin Luther King Jr. had come to Boston to be educated, but he had been assassinated the year I was born and lived on only on the walls of black folks' kitchens and on our church hand fans. The neighborhood had been burned down on the night of his death, and his dream seemed as impossible to me as flying without wings. I had no idea that one day I would be a preacher and travel the world. My whole world was my own small town.

WE ALL HAVE TO SEE BEYOND OUR LIMITATIONS

David was the eighth and youngest son. In his day, youngest sons didn't anticipate a big inheritance. His eldest brother, Eliab, would have received a double portion of the inheritance, with the rest of their father's property divided among the other sons. Given this dynamic, David could not have dreamed that the riches of an entire kingdom would be at his disposal; such thoughts would have been beyond the scope of his imaginings. He probably would have seen his future only within the framework of how he saw his family, neighbors, and town. Growing up, my world was made up of my mother and sister. My father had separated from my mother while she was still pregnant with me, taking both his voice and his financial support away from us in the early part of my life. I was the only boy in our small family and the youngest of the siblings. That was all I knew; I could not even imagine any other life.

The television shows of my childhood that depicted the happy, intact nuclear family were as foreign to me as if they had been beamed from Mars. Their full tables and manicured yards adorned by white picket fences were as unreal to me as the space-age cartoons that played out on the small black-and-white television my mother bought secondhand. The only home I knew was the government-supported housing development with its hot, cramped apartments and urine-soaked, graffiti-covered hallways. Fatherlessness was so normal in our neighborhood that none of my friends had a father in the home either.

We may not have had the wide-open spaces of rural America, but we did the same things as other small-town kids, just with a different ingenuity. We played stickball in vacant lots and fashioned basketball hoops from old milk crates attached to telephone poles. Between the passing of cars, we pretended to be Magic Johnson and Michael Jordan. We also smashed cans into tight cylinders to use for soccer. This was the inner-city version of Little League. The only rainbows I had ever seen as a boy were the oil-slick rainbows left in the gutters of the Roxbury streets. Our beaches were the sizzling-hot blacktop streets. In the summer, the older boys would open a fire hydrant and we would run and scream in the cool water until the fire department showed up to end our fun.

My world was impoverished, but I barely noticed because everyone around me was also poor. When you have never seen anything else, your own deprivation becomes normalized. At least our family was small. Many other poor families on our block were much larger, and they struggled to keep food on the table. Our food shortage came at the end of the month when we ran out of food stamps. Looking into an empty refrigerator as a child, I never could have imagined that one day I would oversee a church food bank that feeds more than fifty thousand people annually. In the same way, the boy David could not have imagined himself as a king with thousands of troops at his command, overseeing the entirety of a unified Israel, particularly when having a king in Israel was still a new concept.

David's childhood world consisted of his father, his father's house, and his father's sheep. He likely heard stories of prophets and kings but never expected to see them, much less live and walk among them. Perhaps that is why David's sheep were so valuable to him: they were all he had. He valiantly chased down wild beasts to rescue them at great risk to himself. But when your world is so limited and lacking, you dangerously defend what little you have.

I have seen this now across the world, from misguided gang members who kill for street corners they do not own to homeless people who fight over boxes to sleep in. I have seen wars fought between cousins over plots of land that were abundant enough to share. I have seen sainted church mothers ready to go to blows over the loss of a familiar seat in the padded church pew and coworkers who backstabbed each other over corporate positions that were later downsized.

This ferocity is what we see in David as he developed his skills. He had a reckless dedication to his sheep, not understanding that his life was far too valuable to be risked. He remained trapped in this mind-set until later in life, when his servants had to rescue him from his last giant and then refused to allow him to go out to battle anymore (2 Sam. 21:17). David risked everything to protect what was his, but that bravery was not tempered by the knowledge of how valuable he was to the whole nation until much later. We, too, often live recklessly because we have no sense that there is a greater good and a greater life coming.

When I was a young minister, I ventured out at midnight to share Christ with the gang members of my city. Many times at knife- or gunpoint, I declared the beauty of the good news, even daring rage-filled gang members to send me to a martyr's reward. When I married and had children, I quickly ended that practice, recognizing that my life had far more value to my wife and children on earth than it would in heaven.

David did not know that one day his bravery would empower him to defy a giant and stand against the enemies of Israel. But already in his small world of Bethlehem, there was a tiny seed of his divine life purpose. There was a king in this kid. David the king would shepherd the entire nation like the dutiful shepherd boy in Bethlehem. He would see peace established through armed struggle and wrestle his nation from the mouth of the ravenous Philistines, just as he did with the lambs of his father's fold.

Sometimes deep devotion is produced out of less-than-optimal circumstances, for it is in places of emotional pain and rejection that we learn to rely on God. In the broken and hurt places in our own hearts, God's love comes to mend the cracks and heal the harms. In his Bethlehem, we can see a boy who was brave but forgotten, valiant but undervalued. Perhaps this was the perfect situation in which to foster a king.

Your Bethlehem experience is necessary to your development because in this sparse and limited environment, you discover who you really are. In Bethlehem, you don't have a collection of tools to work with, so you must make do with what is available. You don't have a team or staff available for support, so you learn how to pray and call out to God to guide you when you face outlandish odds. David discovered how to accurately wield his slingshot in Bethlehem using only the smooth stones pulled from the ground at his feet. In Bethlehem, David learned how to sing and play the music that would usher him to his next city and one day earn him the title of "Sweet Psalmist of Israel." It was in Bethlehem that he developed a prayer and devotional life that would one day be so contagious that it would inspire a whole nation to prayer and praise. Bethlehem is where David found a devotion that would drive him to build a temple for the God he so desperately loved.

Bethlehem was essential to David's spiritual formation, and I believe that our own Bethlehem experiences are vital to ours as well. In loneliness and fear, I learned to pray as a little boy. I learned to praise on an empty stomach, and I developed many of the spiritual skill sets that I still use to this day. Don't despise your Bethlehem, for royalty is birthed in small towns.

2

GIBEAH

The City of Exposure

Just three miles north of Jerusalem, there is a hill called Givat Shaul (literally the hill of Saul). This hill stands some 2,700 feet above sea level, making it one of the highest summits in the region, located along the central Benjamin Plateau. In modern times, the town is called Tell el-Ful, but most biblical scholars have identified this place as the biblical city of Gibeah—King Saul's capital city.

Gibeah was an unusual place to build a capital city for a Benjamite king, as it was here, according to Judges 19 and 20, that the men of the tribe of Benjamin committed a terrible crime. This story depicts a period when there was no king in the land of Israel. During this time, a man from the tribe of Levi, along with his wife (from the tribe of Judah), traveled from her hometown of Bethlehem to return to Mount Ephraim. Because they were setting out late in the afternoon, they had been counseled to stop in Jerusalem, just six miles along their journey. But they decided to pass by the city of Jerusalem (then called Jebus), which was still inhabited by Canaanites. The Levite man decided to travel about four more miles north to find refuge in the company of fellow Israelites.

By sunset, the sojourning couple arrived in Gibeah. There they met an old man who happened to be from Mount Ephraim. The kind old man took the travelers to his home, washed their feet, fed them well, and cared for their animals. But late in the evening, a violent band of Benjamite men from the city overran the house where they were lodged. They raped and brutalized the Levite's wife. These Benjamite men of Gibeah so abused her that she fell dead the next morning on the threshold of the door. Her husband took her body and cut it into eleven bloody pieces and sent one part to each of the other tribes of Israel along with a report of what had occurred in Gibeah.

When the other tribes learned of this crime, the wrath of the entire nation was brought down upon the sons of Benjamin. The other tribes called up an army, and the Benjamites, refusing to turn over the guilty men or acknowledge the sin in their midst, also rallied troops. In the meadows of Gibeah, the two armies clashed, engaging in a bloody battle of brothers, resulting in the deaths of more than twenty-five thousand men of the tribe of Benjamin (Judg. 20:35). Later, in this same battle, another eighteen thousand men of Benjamin were surrounded by soldiers from the other tribes and were taken down with ease, also meeting their tragic end in Gibeah. Amazingly, it is from this bloody place and from this decimated, disgraced, and downtrodden tribe that God called his first king: Saul, son of Kish.

Saul was born in Gibeah and chose to build his castle over-looking these very meadows where his brothers, cousins, and uncles had died. Perhaps it was to be a solemn reminder of how much these people needed a king in their lives. To be lawless and leaderless is a setup for disaster. Although only a few Benjamites decided to break the laws that God had given to Moses, their fellow tribesmen refused to condemn their actions and instead took up arms to defend the criminals. This brought widespread destruction to the entire tribe, such that the tribe was nearly wiped out.

Just as the Israelites needed a king, we all need the lordship of Christ Jesus to reign in our lives. Too often we defend the wrong we do in our lives instead of admitting our errors and surrendering the foolish actions that have brought down judgment. This is dangerous, for grace can come only to those who discern that they need it. Saul built his capital city in this place of past rebellion, and from it he ruled an entire nation. God did not reject this city; rather He promoted it. What we know from the story of this city is that God's wrath is never eternal and His grace is so amazing that He not only forgives but also restores. He not only restores but also promotes.

We will see through David's time at Gibeah that there are stages in our lives when God puts us in places or circumstances that may not seem to make sense for accomplishing our calling. Yet these places are important because they are part of God's plan for developing us and making us ready for the time when we do step into our purpose. From the ashes of Gibeah, God allowed Saul to build a grand city. He used a cursed location to bless a nation.

EXPOSURE FOR PREPARATION

As a boy, David was summoned to the capital city. However, he was not invited to Gibeah to fulfill his calling: stepping into his anointed position as king. It was not his gift of prophecy but rather his gift of service that brought him into the royal court.

King Saul had become a demonized king. The spirit of the Lord had departed from him, and he was plagued by another. Saul was desperate for an anointed minstrel to sing and play until this evil spirit that had come to torment him went away. "And so it was, whenever the spirit from God was upon Saul, that David would take a harp and play it with his hand. Then Saul would become refreshed and well, and the distressing spirit would depart from him" (1 Sam. 16:23 NKJV).

Saul's problem created an opportunity for David to be exposed to royalty to learn more about his purpose. Exposure is important because it shows us that the impossible is possible. David was young, but he could see that someone like Saul—someone from a much smaller, more troubled, and less respected family line in Israel—could become king. He also was able to see that it was possible to redeem a cursed city for a greater purpose. David would go on to do these same things when he became king. Through exposure to Saul, David was being developed as a great leader; he was being prepared for assuming the role God had anointed him to have. And it was important that he spend this time in Gibeah learning lessons he would need later on.

Learning What to Do

In his time with Saul, David learned that even when one's family has some skeletons in its closet—an issue that would follow David throughout his life—an individual can be chosen to be royalty and serve his or her people and God well. Saul showed David the spiritual importance and the power of music to dispel the demonic. This would be a key lesson for David, as he later wrote psalms to express his love for God, to praise Him, and to purge his heart of all that troubled him. He also erected a tent for the ark of the covenant in his own royal city and commissioned musicians to sing in this tabernacle day and night.

David might have felt impatient about having to bide his time playing and singing for Saul when he knew he was anointed as the next king. It was probably difficult to be in Saul's court and keep quiet about his destiny, but David was learning while he waited.

Learning through Service

In the fall of 1987, the church I belonged to in Boston brought me on staff as the new assistant youth pastor. The position came with no salary, but I was honored to serve in that role. The church had yet to purchase or build a sanctuary and was leasing an old theater to hold Sunday morning services. It was my job to pull out and arrange the chairs for the youth group, so I would arrive early enough to carry the folding chairs up the stairs to the balcony hallway before the teenagers arrived. After the service, I promptly packed up and carried the chairs back down the stairs before the adult service was dismissed.

I took attendance and called the youth throughout the week. I typically was asked to speak one Sunday a month, but more often if the lead youth pastor was out of town speaking. I was the chief administrator and ground organizer. I oversaw the volunteers and administrated our little department. I had a job outside the church that paid well for my young age, so I often underwrote our activities from my own checkbook. Responsible for making sure the youth pastor's vision came to fruition, I was dutiful and dogmatic in that regard. I taught our class of sixty-five teenagers perhaps a dozen times a year, but I understood I had not been brought to that position to teach, nor to cast vision; I was brought to that position because I could organize, strategize, recruit volunteers, and run teams.

I had recognized my calling to preach and teach since I was a small boy, but I knew that for this role, my other gifts were more important. I just served in the role I had been assigned and waited for my opportunity. I learned through that experience the importance of never announcing yourself until you are ready to fight a giant. As it turned out, the development of my gifts during that time opened the door to future opportunities.

Eventually, the youth pastor recognized that I was anointed to fill that post. He moved into more of an evangelistic role in our church, making room for me in the unpaid position as lead youth pastor after I had been serving faithfully as his assistant for a number of years. Even with the promotion, however, I still set up and took down chairs. I still called teenagers throughout the week, kept attendance, and organized volunteers. Those gifts got me into the room, so I did not want to stop doing the things that brought me into the circle of my destiny.

Sometimes we are so preoccupied with looking for perfect doors that we miss our moment. God often uses imperfect-looking openings; yet the door that is unlocked is the best door, even if it is just made of pine while the others are gold. As I look back on my life, I see that in many cases the situations that brought me the most advancement in my life were not glamorous or appealing. In fact, they were complicated and unattractive. But the difficulty created a need for my skills and gifts that would not have existed had the situation been ideal or perfect.

People miss opportunities to be exposed to a preview of their own destinies because the invitation seldom arrives in an embossed envelope. Exposure usually comes with no trumpeters and is housed in a role so far from the expected position that it can easily be missed. Exposure most often comes wrapped up in service. Work is not a curse; it is the opportunity to learn and see new things. Being willing to serve gives access and insight many people are secretly craving.

David learned in his time with Saul what is possible when God has anointed a person or a situation. Possibly the most important lesson he learned was to wait on God's timing and trust that he was exactly where he needed to be to prepare for his future. He might have been anointed, but it wasn't time for him to step into that role. He wasn't ready.

Learning What Not to Do

Saul had become a demonized sovereign abandoned by God to the point that the prophet Samuel was commanded by God not to pray for him. This does not sound like the best training David could have had or the kind we would expect God to provide for someone so important to Israel, but David received good lessons through his exposure to Saul. He experienced what it looks like when God has abandoned a king to his own earthbound sovereign will. He saw where the path of free will could take a king. He learned what not to do from the fallen Saul.

David prayed in Psalm 51:11, "Do not cast me away from Your presence, and do not take Your Holy Spirit from me" (NKJV). These words have great meaning to us when placed in the context of what David had seen transpire in Saul's life. Sometimes we complain about how bad things are, but God might be using the "badness" of the situation to give us exposure to the next level.

Have you ever tried to piece together a massive jigsaw puzzle without looking at the box it came in? The cover of the box shows a picture of what the finished puzzle is supposed to look like. You look closely at the picture to get a general idea of how the pieces fit together. But one of the most helpful ways to get started is to find the corners and the edges of the puzzle. Then you fill in the picture from there.

Saul by no means provided for David a perfect picture of a godly king, but he was the closest thing young David had ever seen. In that respect, Saul provided the outline of this picture of kingship so David had some frame of reference.

How many people have you been exposed to who helped define the outline of the puzzle of your destiny? Perhaps the supervisor on your job seems lazy to you, always shirking his responsibilities. Or you might have a teammate who is constantly slacking off. You may not have the perfect boss or the most cooperative team, but these people provide the "borders" for the picture of your future. It is up to you to fill in the details that make up the picture based on what you learn from them. The people in your life may not be the perfect Christians, parents, or mentors, but even in their human and fallen states, they can instruct you. If you reject the examples God has provided, you might end up missing a key lesson He wants you to learn. Even your deficient role models are valuable if they help eliminate some of the guesswork or in some way expedite your development.

Keep in mind that your company may be filled with problematic people, but that's why they need you. Your family might constantly frustrate you, but God providentially placed you in that family to be part of the solution to problems and a witness for Christ. You may be surrounded by incompetent people, but incompetence makes competence necessary.

Learning through Contrast

Growing up in the inner city, I could never really see the stars. A few would make their appearance each night in competition with the lights of the city, attempting to twinkle in the smog-filled sky, but they were not easy to see. Boston also has more than its share of cloudy evenings, and there were many nights when the stars were not visible at all. I had no idea why scientists called our galaxy the Milky Way. The name was totally lost on me because my exposure was so limited.

Now that I live in the Rocky Mountain region of the United States, I can often be found on my back porch with my feet by the evening fire. On clear nights, I stare up into the sky and watch the milky myriad of twinkling lights. I truly appreciate those evenings because in the beauty of our galaxy, I see the declaration of the glory of our God.

I wonder, however, if I would appreciate its beauty as much had I grown up under this sparkling sky. Would my perspective be the same had I not been limited in my exposure? The exposure to the negative was just preparation for the exposure to the positive. Bad things, people, and experiences don't have to be bad if you allow them to teach you to truly appreciate the good. After all, diamonds are best examined when placed against dark backgrounds. I appreciate the majesty of a star-filled sky because I grew up under one that barely held a twinkle.

God will expose you to people who have callings similar to your own or experiences you can learn from. These people will provide instruction for you on either what to do or what not to do, and both lessons are equally important. People instruct us without trying, and they equip us to make our own assessments of their choices and the results.

So thank God for those people. While you are in this stage of life, take every opportunity to learn all you can. Walk around the halls of the palace and learn as much as your heart and head can retain. You may need these insights to build your own fortress in the future. You may need to know how a palace should be constructed and how a royal court should be maintained.

EXPOSURE FOR INSIGHT

God camouflaged David, anointed to be the next king, as a lowly minstrel. No sword was needed for this job, not even a sling. A time would come when these skills would be important in his journey, but there was a great deal he needed to learn. He had to understand more than just the mechanics of utilizing a slingshot or how to wear a crown and sit on a throne; he needed to learn what truly makes a good leader and the importance of relying on God for guidance.

When God is exposing you to your true calling, He will access your lesser calling and employ your other gifts to provide experiences and opportunities. These are just as important—sometimes more important—for exposing you to insight that will make you the most effective when it is time to use your greater gifts.

Creating a Vision of the Future

When I was thirteen years old and in the eighth grade, I won one of the Freedom House student awards for the year. The Freedom House is a civil rights organization that promotes education and community development in Boston. I had pecked out a speech on an old Remington typewriter my mother had bought at a second-hand store to help me overcome my dyslexia. I wrote on the role young people should play to shape the future of their communities, and then I memorized every word. That speech, which I wish I had today, won the award.

The day of the awards ceremony, I recited my speech in front of a small crowd of proud family members and other student winners, as well as a few local political activists, educators, and black business leaders. Upon receiving my certificate, I got a standing ovation from the crowd. For me that would have been more than enough, but the award also included the chance to meet and shadow the owner of the local black-owned music station, WILD AM. This was the station the cool middle schoolers played on their boom boxes in the back of the school bus.

In those days, East Boston had a population that was predominantly Italian American, so the courts ordered that black kids from our neighborhood had to be bused into their neighborhood to promote equal opportunity and access. I think WILD provided the soundtrack for our blackness and our bravery, helping to stave off our anxiety about going into an area that was not always welcoming to blacks. The owner of this station was a local icon, and I was overawed to meet him.

His name was Mr. Nash, and when he shook my hand at the awards ceremony, I had no idea I was being given a glimpse into my own future. This round-faced black man towered over me. His movements were quick but calm, and in a confident, clear voice he introduced himself and gave me his business card. This was the first business card anyone had ever given me. He looked into my wide brown eyes and said, "Now, Chris, you call me at the radio station, and we'll schedule a time for you to come down to see what we do."

In a voice I felt was far too high for a boy, I said, "Yes, sir," and then walked the four blocks back to our apartment on Wilder Street still on cloud nine. The following Monday, I pulled out that business card and called the radio station. I told the receptionist who I was, and to my utter amazement, I learned she was expecting my call to schedule time with Mr. Nash, the local legend. A few days later, I excitedly headed to the radio station. I took the

MBTA bus down to Dudley Square, got off close to the building that housed the station, and went in. Mr. Nash came out quickly and greeted me. Then he showed me all around his station and introduced me to his employees, both on-air personalities and the administrative people. He told me about the makeup of his audience and his constant need to sell advertisements to keep the station alive. Most important, he told me of the power of having a dream.

Mr. Nash influenced my life that day, and neither of us knew how much. He showed me that someone like me could run his own business and help people by creating jobs. He quietly conveyed that even someone who looked like me deserved to have a voice in the world and that this voice could be heard. He demonstrated to me that not all men needed to be violent to have power and that the greatest crime was not trying to do better.

I spent less than two hours with Mr. Nash, but he left his fingerprints on my soul. Neither Mr. Nash nor I knew I would one day be blessed to broadcast our church's Christian radio show, *The Higher Level*, into more than two hundred nations each week. Neither of us could have known then that I also would have a television and sound recording studio and that I would be blessed to provide jobs in my own community. But God knew. He knew I needed to see a man like Mr. Nash succeeding to help me believe I could do similar things.

God orchestrates our steps so we can have these moments of exposure, because even the briefest moment can leave a soul impression that causes our hearts to believe what the Spirit says about us.

Predictive but Not Restrictive

The prophet Samuel told David in Bethlehem that he would be king one day: "The LORD said, 'Arise, anoint him; for this is the one!' Then Samuel took the horn of oil and anointed him in the midst of his brothers; and the Spirit of the LORD came upon David from that day forward" (1 Sam. 16:12–13 NKJV). But we know that the prophecy did not come to fruition until much later, after David's exposure to Saul when he was called to service in the royal court. Prophecy always precedes exposure. God will often reveal things in advance so we won't miss the opportunity for exposure when it arrives.

Exposure is predictive but not restrictive. Just because I have been exposed to someone doesn't mean I am to become just like the person. Exposure is simply a nudge in the right direction. Whether I must learn from what this person has done correctly or incorrectly, exposure is God's way of imparting valuable lessons.

Throughout Scripture, we see examples of how God used exposure to lead His servants in a particular direction, including,

- Esther's being exposed to Mordecai (Esther 2)
- Joshua's being exposed to Moses (Exod. 17)
- Elisha's being exposed to Elijah (2 Kings 2)
- Ruth's being exposed to Naomi (Ruth 1)

Had Esther not been raised by Mordecai, would she have thought herself acceptable to a king? "Mordecai told them to answer Esther.... 'Yet who knows whether you have come to the kingdom for such a time as this?'" (Esther 4:13–14 NKJV). Exposure is God's tool to open our minds to new opportunities and see that nothing is impossible. Esther overcame fears and took on risk to save her people from destruction.

Moses taught Joshua that slaves can be generals and that bodies of water can be traversed without a boat. God wanted to make sure Joshua didn't miss what He was teaching him through Moses, so He instructed Moses to write it down: "Then the LORD said to Moses, 'Write this for a memorial in the book and recount it in the hearing of Joshua, that I will utterly blot out the remembrance of Amalek from under heaven'" (Exod. 17:14 NKJV). These revelations allowed Joshua to lead his people into the Promised Land and back to the faith they had abandoned.

Elijah exposed Elisha to the strange reality that if he struck the water of the Jordan River, it would be divided. Elisha used this lesson when his master was taken up in a chariot of fire. "Then he took the mantle of Elijah that had fallen from him, and struck the water, and said, 'Where is the LORD God of Elijah?' And when he also had struck the water, it was divided this way and that; and Elisha crossed over" (2 Kings 2:14 NKJV). Elisha saw many miraculous things in his time with Elijah, and as that gift was passed to him, he performed many miracles of his own to help his people.

Naomi exposed Ruth to God and the customs of the Jews. "She said, 'Look, your sister-in-law has gone back to her people and to her gods.' … But Ruth said: 'Entreat me not to leave you, or to turn back from following after you.… Your people shall be my people, and your God, my God" (Ruth 1:15–16 NKJV). In exposing her, Naomi ushered Ruth into the family line of Jesus. Even though Ruth was from Moab, a heathen people with a shameful past, she became part of the royal line.

Exposure for Abundance

The discipline to serve without having to announce one's destiny to others is vital to success. I believe that this discipline showed up in the life of David because he had complete confidence in Samuel's prophecy. Saul was not yet ready to acknowledge the "king" in David. In fact, things got dangerous for David when Saul saw in him a potential rival to the throne. David stayed in his role and played his harp, choosing not to proclaim what he knew his eventual destiny to be. He stayed quiet until he was mature enough to handle the backlash that would come from being a threat to the king.

Whenever God gives you the gift of exposure, He is giving you a compliment. He is saying you can do more than you thought and fly higher than you believed possible. Instead of shaking your head and doubting yourself, take this as a sign that your potential exceeds your initial expectations. This is a signal of God's love and regard for you because He believes you will learn from the exposure. He exposes us to what He has purposed ahead of time, knowing we are not yet prepared to step into our ultimate destiny.

Gibeah was a city with a troubled past and home to a troubled leader. By sending David to Saul's court, God prepared him for the immense responsibility he would soon take on. This was an opportunity for exposure to the different paths he could choose as a leader. By learning from Saul's positive and negative examples, David realized the results he could achieve based on his choices.

God gives each of us those same opportunities. We have the gift of seeing where different choices and behaviors can lead us if we pay attention to our own exposure: preparation, insight, and abundance. God does not anoint us with a purpose without equipping us to accomplish it. What is He showing you through your exposure?

VALLEY OF ELAH

The City of Transition

Imagine if your daily life came with a narrator—a baritone off-screen voice announcing the events of your existence, just like in the movies. What if the voice followed you, the plucky protagonist, wherever you went and you could hear the running commentary in your ears? In some cases, it might be annoying, especially if you heard descriptions of every little breath and every mundane task. But it would be motivational to have an omnipresent narrator helping you understand the importance of your actions moment by moment. Having this perspective, ordinary moments would no longer feel tedious and trivial.

I imagine that David would have benefited from a life narrator. After all, he was called back to his first city of Bethlehem to resume caring for his father's few sheep. This must have been very confusing, because he could not know how this would fit into his future. In the midst of one of those seemingly ordinary days, his father, Jesse, asked him to take some food to his brothers who were serving King Saul at the front lines of the battlefield. David left his beloved sheep with an attendant and headed off on this journey to the valley of Elah. What he encountered in the valley would be the public turning point of his young life. That is where he would encounter his first giant.

JUST AN ORDINARY DAY

David's willingness to be obedient in accomplishing a task and serving others opened another door for him to move from his previous city into his next city. The same is true for us: God allows many doors to be available to us, but most of those doors of opportunity are unlocked only by our willingness to serve. Service not only gives us access and exposure but also can ensure that we are in the right place at the right time to receive the right blessing.

The Philistines had drawn battle lines against the children of Israel. As Saul prepared for war, the peace David brought him was not a priority, so David was sent back home. Word went out through the tribes that Saul was calling up the able-bodied young men, including David's brothers, to join his ranks. The Philistine raiders intended to set up towns in the territory of Israel.

The Philistines were not new to Israel, but this was the first time they were mentioned in David's story. His life was punctuated by Philistines and giants. David's first military battle was with a Philistine giant, as was his last (2 Sam. 21:15–22). They were invaders from the island of Crete and factored heavily in David's life. He was a warrior from his youth until the day he was forced by his own men to quit the field of battle, and his life was defined more by what he was fighting than by anything else. But David had no living narrator on this day in Bethlehem to tell him he would face his first giant. There was no commentator to tell him he would face the Philistine army or that life as he knew it was about to change completely.

David seemed to be having an ordinary day, but because each moment is always birthing the next, there really are no ordinary days. Our days are not ordinary either. Each moment is pregnant with potential. We just don't have that narrator to tell us we are constantly living in the city of transition and the valley of change. There are no ordinary days, no ordinary moments. How we choose to live those moments determines the outcome of each day.

THE ARROW PRINCIPLE

Have you ever seen an arrow in the hands of an archer? Invariably the archer must draw the arrow backward—placing it under pressure and pulling it into tension—in order to see the arrow fly. Sometimes God will pull you backward, as He did with David, just to prepare you to fly forward. The pressure and tension are both needed to fuel your flight; the greater the tension, the greater the velocity. The more "backward" you feel in that process, the higher you will eventually fly. I call this the "arrow principle," and I have seen it active in the lives of many people I have pastored over the years. With God, a backward move is not necessarily negative. He might be testing to see if you can handle a promotion. If you can submit to the process of seemingly losing ground, you will be ready to gain so much more.

Margaret is one of the wonderful women in my Denver church. Some years ago, her ex-husband fell sick and needed someone to care for him. Margaret had been estranged from her ex-husband, and her life had gone in another direction entirely, but when their children informed her of the situation, she committed to seeking God's will. In prayer, she felt the Holy Spirit leading her to help her ex-husband, so she promptly rearranged her life, career, and goals in order to fully assist him. Many of her friends and family members thought she was crazy to put her life on hold and "go backward" to care for him, but Margaret felt this was the right thing to do. With unwavering faith in God, she took the risk of putting her own life on hold to serve this man.

Many Sundays I would see Margaret help her ex-husband into our services. She would sit beside him to ensure he made it to church and heard the Word. She got him to his numerous hospital visits on time, prepared his favorite meals, and even made sure his bills were paid and up to date. She also spent endless hours researching the many governmental and hospital programs available to him. She sat on hold for hours, navigating elaborate government phone trees. Margaret patiently debated with customer service representatives and explained the case over and over. In time, she helped to construct a system of support for him that would make his last years comfortable. She totally surrendered her own life goals for a season to benefit him, and I was amazed by her Christian example. She is one of the unsung heroes who have helped frame my own views of what being a real Christian looks like in practice.

Soon Margaret had amassed files full of contacts, phone numbers, and resources that could help people in various crises.

She didn't limit her research to simply what was helpful to her situation; she retained all the information she gathered because she knew that other people would need help navigating the oceans of red tape and bureaucracy she had traversed. And Margaret didn't just collect phone numbers; she made friends in many agencies and organizations.

Today Margaret runs her own successful business (I call it a ministry). She helps connect ordinary people to the resources they qualify for and desperately need. Her "backward" movement eventually propelled her even further. Her sacrifice to benefit another person both sensitized her and equipped her to serve others facing similar challenges. Now she is able to make her living assisting others. Her smile is still infectious and her eyes seem to sparkle even more as she guides many people through the maze of bureaucratic barriers and leads them to the resources they need.

Margaret's experience was like an arrow. Her life seemed to be pulled backward for a while. She endured tremendous pressure as she simultaneously cared for her ex-husband, learned the "system," and managed her personal life. But all that set her up to fly and hit her mark. She moved into another season of her life, with greater service to others.

If you examine your own life, you will see lots of times this arrow principle has been in effect. Backward is not always bad. Sometimes it is the precursor to God's doing something incredible in your life. You are not ready for forward transition until you can pass the test of backward transition. A true servant is comfortable tending kings or tending sheep, and that attitude of submission is vital to future success.

GIANT DOORS

Goliath of Gath was champion of the Philistines. At this point in the history of Israel, it was common in military combat for opposing armies to select a single combatant—one from each side—to represent them. These champions would step forward as the representative of the king and his entire army, and they would fight to a bloody death. Whoever triumphed would be declared the winner, and his army would instantly receive the surrender of the opposing one. This was done to eliminate some of the bloodshed and loss of life that attended these battles. These selected warriors would stand between the two armies, prepared to die but expecting to win. Goliath was well suited to this task. This giant of a man (literally) is estimated by some to have been between nine and ten and a half feet tall and was equipped with a full suit of bronze armor. The spear staff was about five feet long, with an iron spearhead that weighed some fifteen pounds. Taken altogether, his armor and weaponry could have weighed 150 pounds. This man was a walking tank (1 Sam. 17:4–7).

Goliath's name derives from the Hebrew word *golah*, which means "exile" or "migration." This suggests that he was a descendant not of the Philistines but of the ancient biblical race of the Rephaim (Deut. 2:20–21; 3:11). A race of giants that filled the earth before the great flood, they were enormous people and thus became renowned. How these giants resurfaced in the Promised Land is not clearly stated in Scripture, but even before the time Moses led the stunted invasion of the children of Israel in approximately 1400 BC, the presence of the giants there was fully established. These giants caused the Israelites to forfeit their Promised Land for forty years because of their fear of them, and this same spirit of intimidation was active in David's encounter with Goliath in 1025 BC, nearly four hundred years later. Goliath's being ensconced with these Philistines, who were new to the region and invading the land themselves, may indicate that he had somehow "migrated" into their ranks. What king would not want his army to include Goliath, with his great size and strength?

Goliath was not only large but also vocal. For forty days and forty nights, he challenged the host of Israel to send out their champion to do battle with him. For forty days, he intimidated the once-brave soldiers of Saul. It is shocking to me that not even Saul, who stood head and shoulders above the tallest of his troops, would consider taking the challenge. But the king was taken by the same spirit of intimidation that had disabled his troops. Even the king's heroic son Jonathan, who had already demonstrated his prowess, failed to step forward. Goliath caused the bravest of men to tremble in fear just from his size and words.

Before we denigrate Saul, Jonathan, or any of the soldiers of Israel, let's examine our own fears. All of us have been intimidated at times in our lives; we all face and fight fears, whether it is a fear of bees or a fear of dogs.

Some years ago, I taught a series at my church on overcoming fear. I often preach using object lessons, so with this sermon series I brought different kinds of animals into the service to highlight the truth that we are all afraid of something. The back section of my church is a favorite place to sit for a few of the Denver Broncos football players who are members of our church. They can slip in with their wives and children and enjoy the worship, and then they slip out quietly to avoid photo and autograph requests. On one particular Sunday, I was using a twelve-foot-long albino boa constrictor to illustrate my point. I decided to have the professional handler bring the snake through the back door of our sanctuary and stand right by the back section.

You have not laughed until you've seen a huge NFL player who can bench-press a small car jump out of his seat, grab his baby like a football, and take off running down the opposite aisle. It was so funny that I could barely finish the sermon. But I'd made my point: all of us have fears.

To the professional snake handler, the boa was a pet, not a fear. But if I put that skinny veterinarian on a football field and ask him to go against a gigantic NFL lineman, he might have another reaction. Fear is not only powerful but also personal and tailor made for each person, based on one's background and experiences.

To the Israelites, giants were a real and generational source of fear. Their ancestors had delayed their promise over the presence of giants, so why are we so shocked that their sons would have the same reaction to seeing a giant up close? Even their bravest men had to painfully consider taking on Goliath's challenge, and this they did for forty days. So although it is easy for us to castigate them, armed with the hindsight of David's eventual victory, we ought to view them through the lens of our own fears.

King Saul and Prince Jonathan both decided to avoid battle with Goliath of Gath. This uninspiring leadership no doubt strongly influenced the men who had rallied to King Saul's call to arms. When followers see their leaders gripped by fear, the feeling can become contagious, spreading through the ranks.

Instead of seeing this terrifying enemy in front of them, they should have seen this giant as a door to their destiny. The offer of the Philistine king was far too attractive to be ignored. This was the Israelites' first real chance to have the Philistine invaders surrender and submit to them. The Philistines overplayed their hand. The offer they put on the table through Goliath was rather ambitious, but it was the perfect opportunity for the Israelites to have a quick and decisive victory (1 Sam. 17:8–9). If the Philistines honored their pledge, thousands of lives would be saved and peace could be established in the region.

This was risky but certainly worth the king's stepping forward. Yet all Saul could see was the giant, not the door. The doorway to your greatest blessing is often through your most terrifying door. Instead of focusing on the giant, realize that the giant is a door. If the door is that huge, the room itself must be massive. The grip of fear has to be broken, and the reward on the other side of the giant has to be prioritized. One of the meanings of Goliath's name is "migration," and he was indeed David's migration point from being a lowly kid to a lofty king.

How many times have you allowed a door to intimidate you? How many times have you walked away without even knocking? We have to realize that these doors are deliberately designed to be scary because if the door wasn't intimidating, we would all walk easily into our next level—out next city. In fact, the more intimidating the door, the more exclusive the opportunities on the other side of it. Had someone informed Saul that Goliath could have been defeated with one blow, he would have put on his armor and faced him in the valley. But when people aren't confident about the outcome of a battle, they avoid engaging.

Instead of concentrating on the intimidating foe, begin to contemplate the rewards that will come from knocking down that giant. That is a great way to break the hold of fear on your life.

TALKING ENEMIES

Each morning and night, Goliath stood before the Israelite army and issued his challenge. He didn't do this for a couple of days or even a couple of weeks; he did this for forty days and forty nights. This is the same period that our Savior fasted in the wilderness before His face-to-face encounter with the Devil (Matt. 4:1–2). The Holy Spirit led Him into the wilderness to undergo testing before entering public ministry. Additionally, the children of Israel had to wander in the wilderness for forty years before they were able to cross the Jordan and enter the Promised Land. Thus, most scholars consider forty to be a biblical number associated with testing.

Goliath was intent on testing Saul's army. He synchronized his challenges with the rising and setting of the sun, coming first thing in the morning and then again as the sun set. Like a great showman, he took center stage between both armies each day and dared any man to step forward and face him. Goliath knew how to captivate a crowd. No doubt Goliath's challenges dominated the soldiers' conversations throughout the day and continued late into the evening. For forty days, he tested the king and the army of

Israel, and they failed terribly. Goliath didn't lift a finger to fight to achieve intimidation; all he did was talk.

Nowhere in this story do we see Goliath fight. We just hear him talk until the rock strikes him in his huge head. Goliath launched a successful propaganda campaign fierce enough to make brave men freeze in their tracks. His words were more effective than his spear or sword because they paralyzed men—men backed by the Most High God—from even making an attempt to step out in faith. The army listened to the voice of fear until all they believed about God was drowned out.

When the Enemy tries to intimidate you with words, he is trying to drown out your faith. He knows that if you exercise your faith, he will be defeated. In contrast, our Savior went to Calvary without saying any words in His own defense. Like an innocent lamb, He went to the slaughter without saying one word (Acts 8:32). True champions don't need to convince their adversaries that they will defeat them; they just do it. Jesus didn't engage the Enemy in a long dialogue in Gethsemane. In fact, the only words He uttered were not with the Enemy at all; they were all directed to the Father in prayer. Jesus knew that dialogue with a problem just produces fear, but dialogue with one's provider produces faith. Stop listening to your giant and start listening to your God.

WHEN I WIN

David crested the hill in time to hear Goliath's daily tirade, and he heard of the great bounty King Saul placed on the head of the giant (1 Sam. 17:25–27). The man who bested Goliath would be given three things by the king: great riches, the king's daughter's hand in marriage, and freedom from taxes for his family. Any one of these incentives would have made me run for my slingshot, but the soldiers of Israel, including David's three older brothers, were under the spell of Goliath's propaganda. They were so struck by fear and unbelief that they were not moved by these enticements. They said to each other, "What good are riches if you are dead? What good is being betrothed to a princess if you are never able to consummate the union? Better to be alive and pay taxes than to be dead." We are not sure at which point King Saul made these offers. We don't know if he offered them all together at the outset of the challenge or if he started with one and incrementally added other incentives to entice a champion to step forward.

David had not lived under Goliath's manipulation for the past forty days; he was a complete outsider. So when he came over the rolling hill and heard the challenge of the giant, he had only one question: "What do I win when I kill him?" This denoted the transitional mind-set of a person who was moving from exposure to promise—a person who was liberated from fear and walking in faith and ready to realize his potential. This was not an "if I win" mind-set; this was a "when I win" mind-set.

Sometimes God has to select and use outsiders, or at least people who have an outsider's perspective, because their mind-sets have not been tainted by circumstance. David was just the right outsider. He had no armor and no sword. He had a faith-filled mind-set that was not balanced on the knife-edge of "if" but was grounded in the firm foundation of "when."

Too often we allow fear to infect us with an attitude of "if I win." Imagine what would happen if we switched how we spoke and thought about our own future from "if" to "when." If we could conquer our own fears, the level of confidence and release we would experience would be incredible. Giants are defeated in our heads long before they are defeated on battlefields. If we cannot defeat our giants on the battlefields of our own minds, we will never defeat them in the reality of our lives.

FIGHT ON YOUR OWN TERMS

As an outsider, David did not come under the spell of Goliath's taunting and intimidation, but he also did not fight Goliath on Goliath's terms. Goliath was an infantryman. He wore heavy armor and fought with sword and spear. He was ready to face each adversary as the champion of the Philistines' hand-to-hand combat, and it seemed likely he was expecting an infantryman to step from the ranks of the Israelites. But he got David instead: a boy with no sword, spear, or armor. Goliath was insulted by having his challenge answered by such a young and ill-equipped "champion." He expected to face a soldier who would be worthy of his attention.

You can never defeat your first giant by fighting on his terms. David did not approach the giant to clash in hand-to-hand combat; he stayed at the safe distance of a "loser"—the distance of the archer or the hurler of stones. He did not engage Goliath in his kind of warfare. He never allowed him to use the weapons he carried. The only way to overcome the giants in your life is to fight on your own terms.

One of my personal giants was fatherlessness. My father and mother split up before I was born, so I always felt the deep pain of not having my father around. When my closest uncle went to prison, his absence only intensified the emptiness and lack of male role models.

As a young boy, I wondered what kind of man I would be. I dreaded the pattern of crime and abandonment that seemed to plague my entire community and feared it would overshadow my own life. Few of my friends had fathers in their homes, and as I grew up in the government-funded housing developments, the number of men shrank to almost nonexistent. The girls had role models, but the boys had no one positive to look to.

Thankfully, I had been given biblical characters to look to for male inspiration, and they became my role models and heroes—men I could learn about in my little Bible and try to emulate. I came to understand that the giant of fatherlessness would defeat me if I tried to battle it with conventional methods. Without a father, I had to look elsewhere, and most of the men in my community were lacking in their portrayal of masculine excellence.

The apostle Paul is one biblical leader who became a role model for me. He was a clear picture of what it means to be a man. His soaring intellect inspired me to study, and his ability to embrace, decipher, and engage different cultures became my model. Paul was not just a biblical writer to me; he became a life coach and a spiritual inspiration. Paul taught me that it is okay to be smart and that it is possible to be a Christian preacher and still hold a job. He made his tents and preached the gospel, and this dual vocation would frame how I would see myself throughout my life. Even today as a pastor, I have developed outside sources of employment so I would never be totally dependent upon the church to supply the needs of my family.

I also learned from the example of Daniel that strong men stand on their principles. As he faced the threat of being thrown to the lions, he still would not deny his God. I learned from this young Judean that true faith is not up for negotiation and that real men don't back away from what they believe.

Discovering Jesus in the Bible taught me many things, but the message that had the greatest impact was that Jesus cared for His family. From Jesus I learned that real men care for their women. Christ, while dying on the cross, assigned his friend John to watch out for His mother. Our Savior held death at bay long enough to ensure that His mother would be cared for by the youngest apostle (John 19:26–27). This lesson stood in contrast to the culture I lived in each day.

Finally, the three Hebrew boys Shadrach, Meshach, and Abednego also mentored me (Daniel 3). They taught me that real men do not allow the prevailing culture to dictate their decisions. These boys would not defile their faith with the Babylonian culture. Through them I learned that a man could be submerged in another culture and refuse to be changed from what he was taught in the house of his birth. This helped me avoid the gangs that stood guard on every corner of my neighborhood. I refused their drug money and their crime-filled lifestyle because I saw the example of steadfastness in my mentors.

In those days, it was unheard for me to see or even hear from my biological father. Even on my birthdays, when I received cards from "him," I could tell that his signature was in his mother's handwriting. No call ever came from him, and I cannot remember one time he came to our two-bedroom apartment. I knew that one day I would be someone's father and would have to give my children the kind of love I had never received. If I was going to know a father's love at all, it would have to come from my personal relationship with the God of the Bible. Before I was five years old, I began framing my definition of a father based on the God of my Bible. And in my childlike way of thinking, God really became my father. I fully embraced that He was all I had and all I would ever get. This father did not disappoint. He was never late, and He was always with me. He didn't forget birthdays, and He didn't reject the son He'd made. As I pressed into understanding who He was and what He could be in my life, I found myself being healed of the fear a fatherless son has when facing life. I could climb the highest mountain and take a leap of faith because this father would always catch me. Over time I learned that God the Father not only was sufficient but also would supply the only model of a father I would need to one day raise my own sons.

This is the lesson David teaches us at the valley of Elah, the city of his own transition: giants do fall, but only when we use what God has equipped us with.

VICTORIES ON ANY BATTLEFIELD STILL COUNT

When King Saul finally heard there was a volunteer to fight Goliath, he was no doubt intrigued. He had raised the bounty to a level at which any brave man would consider it. Still, he had to be surprised when the handsome but young David was brought before him. Saul was so stressed about the standoff with the Philistines that he did not even recognize David from his time singing at his court (1 Sam. 17:55).

David had to convince Saul to bet on him, and it was a huge bet. Should the agreement be honored between the armies, then the fate of the kingdom would be riding on the outcome of this battle. Saul told David he was too inexperienced and the giant had many more years in battle than David even had been alive. But David began to recount his victories over the lion and the bear in Bethlehem. This retelling convinced Saul to bet on this young man.

Don't be discouraged because you have never won against the current challenge you are facing. Victories won on all fronts still matter. Life is a battle of faith, and if your faith is built up by what you overcame in another area of your life, then draw the memory of that victory into your present struggle. The same God who helped you in your past struggle is able to assist you in your present struggle. He would not have begun something in your life *then* that He can't complete *now* (Phil. 1:6).

David had not killed a giant, but he had faced a lion. By using the crude weaponry of a shepherd boy, he defeated the king of beasts. The memory of that victory gave him confidence that he could defeat the Philistine champion. No one else saw him defeat the lion, but it still counted. Likewise, your private victories are preparing you for public victories. In the battlefield of faith, no victory is wasted.

What battles have you won in your private life? What struggles have you walked away from victoriously? Those struggles required you to be prayerful and brave. Those victories bolster your confidence for when you face your most public giant.

I am so thankful for the private adversaries I had to defeat—my own lions and bears I battled when no one was watching. They taught me I had the internal tools necessary to win and assured me I could not be defeated if God was on my side (Rom. 8:31). I fought them with no television cameras recording, and I fought them long before the invention of social media, but I recorded them in my own mind and heart. I fought them when few people, even in my hometown, knew my name or believed in my potential. God gave me the gift of obscurity so I could prepare for the times when my battles would be more visible and public.

USE WHAT YOU'VE GOT

When you are facing public giants, you must trust not only God but also the weapons (skills and abilities) you are going to use. Saul offered David the armor and sword of an infantryman. David tried on the armor but ended up refusing to wear it, for he had confidence in his skills developed in private struggles. David wanted to use what he knew rather than untried weapons. Going into battle in other people's armor can present unnecessary challenges. God has already prepared you to win with talents He has given you. Learn to use them and be confident in them.

Recently, I was asked to speak at a large church in Texas. The congregation numbers not in the thousands but in the tens of thousands, and the senior pastor is known throughout the world. It was not my first time to preach there, but even after more than twenty years of full-time ministry, I get nervous before I speak. I was just about to leave the pastor's study when a sound technician asked me, "Pastor Hill, would you like to use one of our Countryman microphones that fastens to your head, or would you prefer to use the handheld one?"

Without hesitation, I said, "The handheld, please." I had used a Countryman microphone before, but I had never used theirs. With one hundred thousand people watching the message via the Internet, I did not want to risk speaking with a microphone I had not "proved." Had there been time for a sound check, I would have welcomed the opportunity to use their fancy microphone. But the stakes for me were too high, and I already had butterflies in my belly. After the pastor's warm introduction, I picked up the handheld microphone—the same type I use twice a week in my own pulpit—and started to speak. With God's help, the giant of my own nervousness quickly fell down and I was able to deliver the message the Lord gave me.

In the same way, David rejected the stout armor of Saul. Instead, he went to a brook, picked up five smooth stones, dropped them into his shepherd bag, and headed for battle. David decided to use what was familiar as he faced the giant. We, too, would be wise to use what we know and have tested to bring down our own giants.

SOMETIMES YOU JUST HAVE TO THROW THE BALL

To the cheers of the Israelites and the jeers of the Philistines, David had prepared his sling and taken up his position. Now he was ready to let the rock fly.

Preparation, although critical to success, is anticlimactic if we refuse to "hurl the stone." We will never fulfill our purpose unless we show up for the job interview, audition for the role, try out for the team, or start the new organization. Signing up is not enough; showing up is everything.

All transition requires risk, and David decided to show up. He selected five stones because he was prepared to miss the first shot but was equally determined to take the next one. He was ready to risk hurling a stone at the armored behemoth, and thank God his aim was true. David knew he was in a position of risk, and his selection of four additional stones demonstrated that he was not overconfident. David embraced his moment but with the understanding that something could go wrong. Remember, there was no narrator of David's life. He had not been told by an off-screen voice that he would be victorious, nor had the prophet Samuel sent him an updated message foretelling conquest. No angelic visitation had occurred to proclaim certain triumph.

Life seldom announces our transitional points. All we have is the risk of succeeding or failing. But there can be no forward movement if we are not willing to risk. David followed his routine as if he were going out to tend the sheep, and at the moment of truth he took a risk and hurled the stone.

We all can learn from this brave boy. David challenges us to rely on God's power and protection when we face the giants in our lives. He reminds us that our normal weapons are sufficient for the task. We don't need the updated slingshot; the old one will do fine. We don't need special rocks imported from another country; the local brook is good enough to make stones smooth.

Some years ago, a young man named Onterio Green called me. He had attended my youth group in Dallas and wanted to enroll in the Bible institute where I served as an adjunct professor. The night before he called, he had seen me being interviewed on television. When he heard I was teaching homiletics (the art and science of preaching) at Christ for the Nations Institute, he felt compelled to contact me.

Onterio believed that it was God's will for him to attend the school, and he wanted to know if I could assist him. Having married young and with two children to care for, he did not have much money. Plus, he was not the most studious young person I ever had in my youth groups. But as I spoke to him on the phone, I began to share his belief that God was leading him in this direction. I did not hear an audible voice or receive any overt sign, but I have talked with so many young people being called into full-time Christian ministry that I can almost feel it when it's genuine.

"If you are serious about this, go down to the school tomorrow and apply," I said to Onterio. "Tell them everything you told me, warts and all, especially the part about having no money for school. If God wants this to happen, it will happen."

I was encouraging but did not offer to do the work for him. I don't believe in just opening doors for people who refuse to even knock on them. I told Onterio to call me back after he completed his application, but I made no promise and gave no assurances.

Despite not making any promises, as soon as we got off the phone, I called one of the professors and the dean of the school to see what could be done for Onterio. I had never approached anyone in the school administration like this before, so both of them took me seriously and immediately started to create a scholarship to accommodate Onterio's needs. But I told both of my colleagues not to put anything into motion until the young man submitted his application.

To my great delight, the next day Onterio went down to the office, filled out all the paperwork, and told his story. The administration pulled strings and created a scholarship that would enable him to attend the school. A few years later, Onterio graduated with honors. He currently serves in full-time ministry as the young-adult pastor at The Potter's House in Dallas, the same church where he was raised and came to faith.

Onterio and his wife, Crystal, have told this story many times and give me way too much credit for his admission into Bible school. The real hero of the story is Onterio, because he had no idea my colleagues were working on a scholarship for him. He walked into an office, sat across from a complete stranger, and told his story. He hurled his stone against the giant of rejection.

David took a risk in the valley of Elah, the place where he left obscurity and became a leader. A moment after David hurled his stone, the giant fell face-first in the dirt, as though he were bowing before a king. And the giant was bowing before a king, for David had just taken his first step toward the throne. No longer a harpist only, his true identity as warrior was revealed. Even as the stone made its trajectory, the trajectory of David's life had been forever changed. He would not return to Bethlehem as the same man. He was no longer David the shepherd boy; he was now the champion of Israel.

TRANSITION REVEALS RELATIONSHIPS

David came to the battlefield to pay the family tribute and check on his three older brothers. But when the giant stepped out, David stepped up. It is amazing to examine the reaction of David's oldest brother when David offered to defend the honor of Israel and their God. Eliab viewed David with disdain (1 Sam. 17:28). His tone with his younger brother was belittling, as he essentially said, "Why are you here? You're so arrogant. Who's watching the sheep while you're here?" When David caught the attention of the king, he also caught heat—and hatred—from his brother.

Transition doesn't always change relationships, but it does reveal the true nature of them. When God walks you through transition, expect some of your relationships to change, but don't allow the Enemy to tell you that the transition caused the rift. The transition serves to unearth the feelings another person had toward you all along. Transition is not for the mild of spirit, because great transition will cause friends, coworkers, and even family members to say things you never expected. Transition can cause you to battle not only the giant but also the people who should be standing behind you. When walking through transition, people might question your motives, suggesting you are trying to grab the spotlight. But David's answer to his brother is a great example for us. He said, "Is there not a cause?" (v. 29).

David didn't argue with his accuser. He didn't become defensive or allow his brother's words to make him doubt himself. He just stated that the cause he was taking up was far more important than his brother's opinion. By staying focused on the cause, we can stay on course even when people question or challenge us.

Through David's time in the valley of transition, we can see how the ordinary doesn't have to be mundane. Taking a step backward is often preparation for launching forward, and great challenges usually come before great opportunities. God has equipped us for the battles we will face and is preparing us for them even in these places of transition.

4

JEBUS

The City of Personal Promise

Battle in David's era was bloody and brutal. In modern warfare, a drone, controlled remotely from thousands of miles away, can drop a bomb from the sky on unsuspecting insurgents. But warfare in the Bible was up close and personal. Afterward, the battlefield would be littered with bodies and stained with the blood. Wounded and dying men cried out in pain and desperation. The carrion birds, as if summoned by the sounds of death, filled the air with their own cries, landing on the bodies of the fallen.

This was not the typical milieu in which one would expect to find a boy. David was too young to be called to the battlefield in service of his king, but by the hand of God he had been thrust into the middle of the story and had come of age on the battlefield. Soon enough, David would move on to the city of Jebus, but first he had to conclude his work in the valley of Elah, where he defeated the giant.

The valley of Elah is quite beautiful, situated twenty miles southeast of Jerusalem. It is verdant, with terebinth and oak trees standing guard. On either side of the flat, open fields are stony hills covered with brushwood and dotted with globe thistle and blue lupine flowers. Using imagination, one can envision the tents of the Israelite army still blowing in the evening breeze as Goliath stood crying out for a challenger those forty nights. The setting sun turns his bronze armor into the color of gold. The area between the two rocky hills was small enough that it would have been easy for both armies to see Goliath fall. One can almost hear the Philistines gasp in fear as their champion falls and hear the cries of victory rise from the army of Israel.

Today the topography is still virtually untouched by time, such that standing there brings the biblical story alive. The bloodstains have been worn away by time, but we cannot forget the aftermath of the battle. This would have been David's first time witnessing this type of horror and the first time he would stand in the shadow of death (Ps. 23:4).

David slayed the giant with one smooth stone, but he did not spend a long time reveling in the blessed fortune. He instantly sprang into action, running over to the giant and unsheathing his sword. The Bible says that the stone David slung at Goliath killed him, but David was not satisfied with that. He used the giant's own sword to cut off his head.

DISCARD OLD WEAPONS

David used his sling initially, and it was effective in killing the lion and the bear, as well as his first giant. But as the theater of warfare changed, he put down his sling and picked up a new weapon: the sword. He no longer would face enemies at a distance; he would have to learn how to stand among the rank and file and cut his enemies down with his sword. New situations call for new weapons.

As we face more complex challenges, our tactics and tools must also become more complex. Many Christians have walked with the Lord for many years but have never been taught to develop themselves spiritually. Childlike faith is necessary to enter the kingdom, but over time we must mature in our faith to sustain us as the battles intensify.

In July of 1992, my wife, Joy, and I had just returned from our honeymoon at a borrowed time-share in Aruba. I had moved my new bride and all her things from her college dorm into my one-room bachelor's studio. We made our bed together on my blue college futon as I saved up to buy a proper bed for us. We were so young and in love that the sparseness of our cramped apartment didn't bother us at all. We just giggled like little kids, amazed that we were finally married after our nine-year courtship.

One night after I had fallen asleep, Joy sat up in bed and watched me breathe in my sleep. She reached out to touch me, innocently wanting to caress my shoulder, hardly believing I was there. As her hand touched me, I sprang into action. In one move, I leaped from the bed and somersaulted into the corner of the room. I grabbed a four-foot-long stick that I had propped up in the corner and spun it into a striking position. I was still mostly asleep. I was acting on pure instinct—the instinct of someone who had once had to fight off rats in his sleep. I was just about to bring the stick down on my bride when I caught myself. I was in no danger. I wasn't sleeping outside or under a porch in Roxbury.

My beautiful bride had simply caressed me in our clean, secure apartment in a quiet, safe part of town. It was then that I realized I was still carrying a weapon from my past with me into my future and I no longer needed that instinct or the weapon.

A New Arsenal

The battles in our lives change over time. The challenges we face at one point are very different from the ones we face at others. The struggles will be perpetual until we reach heaven, but the foes we face, the terrain of the battle, and the pace of the battle will change. In the different seasons of life, the weapons we need will change.

In the peaceful times, we can take comfort and rest in knowing we will have our weapons at the ready but will hardly need them. However, in times of intense warfare and struggle, our weapons will be constantly in our grasp.

Prayer

The weapon of prayer will be on our lips, and even our sleep at night will be interrupted by silent cries to God. In times of fierce battle, prayer comes easily, for there are no atheists in foxholes. When life drops bombs on us, prayer becomes second nature.

In the wake of the 9/11 terrorist attacks on the World Trade Center in New York City, the churches of the United States filled to capacity the following Sunday morning. It was not a long-lived season, but although the fear ignited by the attacks persisted, people all over the nation sought the comfort found in prayer. Prayer is a powerful weapon, and we reach for it quickly like a lifesaver when we feel as though life is about to take us under.

The Bible

The Word of God takes on special significance when we face big struggles. The Scriptures give us solace when we are facing grief. Many times in my life, a particular scripture has come to mind that put my heart at ease and calmed the storms raging in my mind. When my father died a few years ago, there really were no words any person could say to stop my heart from hurting. My relationship with him had many levels of complexity and leftover hurts due to his abandonment of us when I was young. No preacher could eulogize away those hurts, and the numerous greeting cards I received, while deeply appreciated, lacked the poetry to capture what I was feeling. But the words of the Bible somehow brought light to the darkness of my grief.

The Bible not only encourages and comforts but also instructs. Its wisdom is so unparalleled that at one time no person in the Western world was considered educated if he or she had not studied its pages. Theology and history clap their hands together in the pages of my Bible and applaud a loving God. Someone formed this acrostic for "Bible": Basic Instructions Before Leaving Earth. That's so true. But the Bible offers so much more than instruction, as it contains God's promises. I have often quoted the promises of God to myself when it seemed my personal world was careening out of control.

I find strength in knowing that God cared enough about us to give us His words of encouragement, instruction, and guidance.

To me, the Bible is proof of His great love for us. It is our ancient love letter, written thousands of years ago, yet it remains more relevant than our next problems.

Worship

There have been times in my life when a spirit of heaviness was so tangible I could almost feel it anchored to my soul. At such moments, even prayer, which is usually like breathing to me, became a struggle because of the intense spiritual warfare and emotional turmoil I was experiencing. Thankfully, I discovered the powerful weapon of worship.

When I've felt as though my prayers wouldn't break through the ceiling, let alone ascend to the heavens to reach God, a song has risen in my spirit that allowed me to penetrate the heaviness. The times I felt too weary to retreat into study of the Scriptures, I found myself singing biblical passages in praise and worship. Using this weapon, the strongholds of depression and sadness fell away.

Friendship

Walking in agreement with close Christian friends is another weapon in the arsenal against darkness. Good Christian friends become invaluable when facing the Adversary because they offer prayer support, biblical guidance, and loving accountability as you fend off his attacks and temptations.

Prayer, the Word, worship, and friends are just four of the weapons available to us. Having unlocked a deeper understanding of them, I've found there are different levels of using them depending on one's maturity as a believer and the type of warfare one is surrounded by. I came to faith in Jesus Christ when I was very young, so I have always prayed. But how I prayed as a child compared to how I pray as I've matured has radically changed. I have studied the Bible as long as I have been able to read, but the meaning and sustenance I receive from it have increased over the years. In fact, it seems the greater the level of need I bring to the Scriptures, the greater my capacity to receive more from them.

I have always worshipped and praised the Lord, but now I crave those private moments of reflection because I find great peace in them. Likewise, I have always been a friendly and outgoing person, but now I make friends intentionally and prayerfully, knowing that I need people in my life who are spiritually aligned with my purpose. These friends are willing to add their weapons to mine in times of intense testing.

I have always used these weapons, but as I have matured, my awareness of the battle raging around me has heightened. As my awareness has increased, so has my need to define and refine these weapons—to learn how to use them biblically to see victory at the next level of my spiritual development.

FOUND WEAPONS

The stick I had in my apartment had been with me for eighteen years. I'd found it the night I climbed out the window of my mother's apartment with the intention of never returning home again. I was only six years old, but our life had become unbearable. My mother had emotionally crashed under the immense pressure of raising my sister and me alone, a fate she had not expected or desired. She had fallen into deep depression and isolation, which translated into physical abuse toward us. My sister, Marie, who is eighteen months older than I, had already escaped out the window one night. She had begged me to run away with her, but I was too loyal to my mother to leave her alone.

Children in traumatic situations sometimes take on caregiver roles when their parents walk through dark times. As the little man of the house, I felt it was my duty to stay and take care of my mom. But once my sister left and I was alone with my mother, things spiraled further out of control. I was left hungry, scared, and worried about the physical abuse. At six years old, I was already tired of being scared of the woman I loved, and I missed the nurturing mother the depression had taken from me. I didn't even know this woman. She was not the strong and determined woman who taught me Bible stories when I was smaller. This was not the happy woman who made up bedtime stories and took us to the library. I cannot describe the thought process of a hopeful six-year-old who has lost all hope.

One night after a terrible beating, I decided to run away. I waited for my mom to fall asleep and then eased the window open, praying that it would not squeak. I had packed a little backpack and put on a warm sweater and my heaviest coat. There was no food in the house, so with no more provision than a toy car and an Incredible Hulk toy stuffed into my bag, I decided to run. I pushed the window open just wide enough for my slim body to slip through and then lowered myself out of our first-floor window.

Holding my breath like a swimmer diving into the ocean, I let go of the windowsill and dropped down into the dark alley behind our apartment.

A year later, I found out that my sister had run to our grandparents' house. She had made her way through the dark streets alone. She was eight years old, yet she had walked one mile through one of the most dangerous neighborhoods of Boston. She had slipped out the window, climbed the fence, walked until she reached our grandparents' green-sided triple-decker, and rang the doorbell.

I was not as fortunate, nor as well informed. I didn't know how to get to my grandparents' house or any of the homes of people we knew. My world as a six-year-old was mostly made up of my mother and sister. I walked into the darkness with no plan as to where I would run. I just knew I couldn't stand to be beaten again. I could not take it another day. As terrified as I was of the dark night, I was more afraid of living with this mother I did not know. I knew that my mom loved me, and I loved her so deeply that I couldn't even imagine spending one night away from her. But I realized that she had been kidnapped by her own sadness and that I needed to get away. I prayed a prayer to Father God as I slid backward out the window.

When my shoes hit the ground, I suddenly realized I didn't know where to go. But I didn't want my mother to see me and perhaps beat me again for attempting to escape, so I walked just a few yards to hide under one of the concrete balconies that lined the back alley of our tenement. In the darkness and cold, I clung to the concrete wall. I cleared away the garbage that had accumulated in the corner and made a little spot for myself. I crouched in the corner and began to cry. Too scared to run out into the night but too frightened to return home, I set my back against the wall and prayed quietly in the darkness. I decided to wait there until morning came and then figure out where to go. I just had to survive the night.

Five feet from my hiding place was a green trash dumpster. It was overflowing with trash bags from all the people who lived in the tenement. The dumpster smelled rank, and a brown greasy sludge pooled on the concrete around it. Rats moved in and out of the holes that rust had made in the bottom of the dumpster. Their feet made splashing sounds as they walked through the sludge. I decided to sleep there for the night, my back against the wall and my knees pulled to my chest.

When I was cleaning out the corner, I noticed a wooden pole on the ground beside me. It was the kind of pole used as a hanging rod in a closet. Almost as tall as I was, the pole was light enough for me to carry. In the darkness, I pulled the stick to me and held it to my chest. In my six-year-old brain, I imagined that an angel had placed this "weapon" there to help me ward off the fear and the rats throughout the first night of my life alone.

Crouched low in the darkness, gripping the stick, I waited for dawn. I sang songs of praise to the Lord, thanking Him for keeping me safe. I kept rocking back and forth to calm myself and keep the rats away from me.

Sometime in the night, I managed to fall asleep with my chin pulled down into my coat. One of the gray rats made its way over and sniffed at my feet. It probably was just curious, but I reacted as though I were under attack. I awoke without making a sound, pulled instantly out of my horrid dreams, and brought my stick down to the ground, striking toward the rat's head. I missed my mark, but my intention sent it scurrying off to easier prey. With my heart beating out of my chest and adrenaline coursing through my veins, I returned to my night watch. Clutching my stick, I cried and prayed till the dawn broke.

As the sun began to rise, I pulled on my backpack, slipped my hood over my head, and walked out of the alley. Though the shadows had been pushed back by the sunlight and I felt safe enough to venture out, I still walked with my stick in hand. And no matter where I lived from that point on, that stick went with me. I had it with me on my yearlong journey of hiding on the streets, and when I was finally found, I took it with me to my aunt and uncle's house in the suburbs. When the courts ordered me out of her house, I brought my stick to my new foster home.

Three years later, my mother had valiantly fought her way back to find herself. On the day a social worker and our court-appointed lawyer returned my sister and me to our mother, I stashed the stick in the same spot where I had found it five years earlier. That night, I snuck out into the alley to retrieve it and brought it into the apartment just in case I ever had to run again.

When I moved out and got my own place at nineteen years of age—eight years later—I still packed that stick with me. It kept guard in the corner of the room beside my bed until the night I almost hit my wife with it. Once useful, the weapon had become outdated.

The next day I walked the stick out to the river flowing behind the rehabbed chocolate factory that housed our small apartment. I watched it wash away, down a waterfall, and out of my life. I would fight more battles in my life, but not with that weapon.

That stick was no longer necessary, as that sad and horrible season of my life was over.

COLLECT THE TROPHIES

David took up the sword of Goliath and cut off his head because there is no need to keep the corpse of a giant once it has been slain. In the battle against our giants, it is necessary to not only defeat them but also dismantle them. The obstacles that have stood against us should be examined after their defeat so we will know they were not as dangerous as we thought.

Goliath was a giant, but he was still a man. The other soldiers of the army of Israel were paralyzed by his taunts for more than forty days and nights before David defeated him. His size, armor, and threats were enough to convince the most valiant soldiers of Israel that Goliath could not be defeated. They might have regarded the giant as more demon than human. David decapitated the giant so all the troops could see that Goliath's power was not supernatural. So often we make the things we fear bigger than they truly are. We imbue natural obstacles with supernatural powers, and the things we are facing become larger than life: they become giants that paralyze us. Once we defeat them, it is important to demonstrate for others that these giants are not supernatural, demonic, or all-powerful; they are just large human problems.

The importance of unmasking these giants is just as vital as defeating them so others' fears will be assuaged. Giants will hold their power unless they are proved not to be greater than we are. When you take on other giants in your life, use this same approach.

For example, when you take on the giant of debt, it is important to also show people that debt is not insurmountable; normal people with simple tools can bring it down. Don't just overcome the giant of depression in silence; stand over this enemy and show the world that depression can be defeated with God's help. Don't just overcome the giant of fear; cut off its head and make it a public spectacle. Gather the public trophy to the power of the grace of God that is active in a believer's life. We have to publicly dismantle the mystique of our giants so others will be encouraged to fight their own.

This is why, after all these years of silence on many issues in my life, I am compelled to share. The giants I have faced and overcome have been numerous and terrifying, but I was mistaken not to display their decapitated heads to the body of Christ. It is my hope that these trophies of His grace will encourage others to face their own giants. The giant of fatherlessness, the giant of motherlessness, the giant of physical abuse, the giant of homelessness, the giant of foster care—these have all been slayed with the stones God has given me. Now I am finally in an emotional space where I feel able to allow others to know the details of these hard-fought battles so they will find courage to fight their own enemies.

OFF WITH HIS HEAD

When David removed the giant's head, it was an act that was both significant and symbolic. This was not an easy task for the lad, especially because he had never wielded such a large sword. But David announced to Goliath before the battle that he intended to remove his head (1 Sam. 17:46). The Hebrew word used here is <u>*cuwr,*</u> and it is a primitive root that can be easily translated "turn off." I like that much more than the translation of "take thine head" in the King James Version.

When defeating our giants, we have to not only determine from the outset to overcome them but also turn off the threatening voice that harassed us in the past—to break the inner recording that has intimidated and paralyzed us. We have to turn off the giant's voice and stop it from causing us fear. David also symbolically cut off the mind-set of oppression the giant had imposed on the host of Israel. Even the king and the valiant prince had fallen under its influence. David turned off that way of thinking; he broke the spell. Don't allow threats to continue echoing in the valleys of your psyche; decide to turn them off.

The stick I found as a little boy had ceased to be necessary long before I discarded it. The hairpin reflexes and light sleeping habits I honed in the streets and in foster care had not been needed since I was eleven years old, yet I could leap instantly from a deep sleep well into my twenties, and I was in my thirties before I could walk slowly down a street without looking over my shoulder. The traumas we have survived will blur our perspective of life unless we allow God to clear our vision so we can see what our lives have truly become.

By the time I was eleven years old, the nurturing healthy mother I knew when I was five had been fully restored to me. By the time I was nineteen, I had moved myself into a safe studio apartment in a quiet part of the city. Yet it took me years to turn off the voices that told me I always had to live on high alert, constantly on guard.

Through my years of counseling people, I have prayed with many Christians who have overcome their giants but are still listening to the voices of the dead giants they have defeated. They live still dominated by the mind-set of their oppressive past. For example, a man whose father left him when he was a child still lets that event mar his postive relationships with other men even though he survived the abandonment. A woman whose husband beat her still has him living in her head even though she has long escaped his hurtful hands. A man whose girlfriend broke his heart is still feeling degraded by her even though he has not spoken to her for decades. We have to cut the heads off and turn off the voices if we are to be truly free from their influence. David cut the giant's head off as a sign to us that the battle has not really been won until our giants' voices are removed from our lives.

BURY IT IN YOUR FUTURE, NOT YOUR PAST

After removing Goliath's head, David did something amazing: he "took the head of the Philistine, and brought it to Jerusalem" (1 Sam. 17:54). At the time he did this, Jerusalem was not under the control of the children of Israel. King Saul did not rule in that city. Jerusalem was still controlled by the Jebusites and would stay under their control until King David defeated them in 1003 BC. The Jebusites were the pre-Israelite inhabitants of Jerusalem; they were listed in the outline of nations found in Genesis 10 as a Canaanite tribe that occupied the cities that would become the territory promised to the tribes of Judah and Benjamin. Because the city had the best fortifications of any city in Canaan, and because of the natural positioning of Jebus, Israel was unable to defeat the occupants. Even though the armies of Israel were able to conquer the cities of Jarmuth, Eglon, Lachish, and Hebron, they were not able to dislodge the inhabitants of Jebus (Josh. 15:63; Judg. 1:21).

At the time that David took the head of Goliath to the city, it was not yet called Jerusalem. David did not take the head back to his family home in Bethlehem. He did not take it to the existing capital of Gibeah, where he served King Saul as a minstrel. He took it to the Canaanite city of Jebus, which had not been fully conquered even after the invasion of Joshua, son of Nun, some two hundred years earlier.

Why did David take the severed head, the great trophy of his transition, to this unconquered territory? Because it is important to bury your trophies in your future and not in your past. Even at this young age, David was already dreaming of his conquest of the city.

When you overcome one giant, do not take the trophy to a place in your past. Do not bury the trophy in a territory others have conquered; instead, dream of a new territory of conquest and bury your trophy there. Think about trophies you have for sports or academic competitions. Even your diplomas or other certificates are trophies of victories. Do you leave those at the place where you won them? No. They are displayed on a shelf or a wall where you can see them and draw inspiration from them. In the same way, take the confidence and boldness that come from defeating your giant and do not revel long in the place where you achieved the victory. Start dreaming a greater dream and bury that trophy there.

It is important to celebrate each victory, but not too long. Use the success in one "city" to encourage yourself to set goals that are years and even decades ahead of you. Having a future goal keeps you on your knees in prayer and causes you to stretch yourself constantly to be the best version of you that you can be. The foresight David displayed is truly remarkable. He had prophetic insight of his own future as he planted the head of Goliath in the city he one day intended to conquer and establish his dynasty in. At that young age, having just won his first military battle, David was already dreaming of conquering the most fortified city in the region.

The questions become, What are we dreaming about and praying about? How much time have we spent in prayer so we can discern God's will for our lives? How far are we able to "see" ourselves in the future? Samuel was not present on the battle-field—there was no prophet available in that moment—but David had his own "inner prophet," and we need to develop this ability also. We should learn to seek God to know His divine destiny for our lives. David showed us that it is possible to set a goal twenty years before the manifestation of an event and watch it unfold.

I meet so many people who have stopped dreaming. Life can be challenging on a day-to-day basis. The drudgery of paying bills, meeting deadlines, and running errands can cause us to forget our dreams. Remember what you used to daydream about when you were seventeen? Maybe you were sitting in your math class and the teacher was explaining some arcane equation and your mind was a million miles away. What were you seeing? Who were you in those dreams? More important, where did you bury those hopes? Too often, instead of burying our trophies in the soil of our future, we bury them in the graveyard of our past. We need to dig up those childhood dreams and teenage visions we have discarded. When I am counseling people, I often ask them, "Who were you before you buried your dreams?" I challenge them to remember who they were before the pain, challenges, and disappointments of life began to steal their ability to believe in their dreams.

When you bury your trophies in your future, you are creating a shield against discouragement and a wall against defeat. You are building assurance that your past victories are a foreshadowing of future victories. You are saying to the giants in your future that you are ready to use the inspiration of past victories to seal the deal.

CHANGE THE NAME

David was still a teenager and would not conquer Jebus for another twenty years or so, but he had already changed the name of the city. He called Jebus "Jerusalem" because he had already declared his intentions. In the same way, we have to speak the future we are desiring to see, even in the face of our current situation. We need to rename things in our lives, in bold faith statements, trusting that God is able to change them.

Stop calling your cities blighted and start calling them blessed. Stop calling your personal life defeated and start calling it victorious. Stop saying that your best days are behind you and start declaring they're yet to come. By changing the verbiage about your situation, you are expressing faith in the Word of God over your life. You are rehearsing the personal promises and prophecies that have been spoken over you.

MY OWN JEBUS MOMENT

When I was twenty-two years old, I began to fall in love with praying in the early mornings. The church I attended and served in opened its doors for prayer each morning at five. As I developed the discipline of prayer, I learned to spend most of my mornings walking the floor of the prayer chapel and calling on the name of the Lord. In time, the pastoral leadership noticed my faithfulness to prayer and gave me keys to the church. I would arrive earlier in the winter months to fire up the furnace so the older parishioners would be warm when they were kneeling in prayer. I would roll out of bed at four in the morning, shower, and then drive my car through the dark, snowy streets to open the doors and turn on the heat. I learned to love the ritual and to be of service to the elder church members.

One morning as I opened the church, I kicked the snow off my boots, turned on the lights, and fired up the furnace. I walked in and made my way to the pulpit. For the first time, I prayed that God would allow me to serve Him by being a pastor. The people of this church had no idea I had been a child preacher. They did not know I had been told by many godly people I respected that I would one day preach the gospel globally. To them, I was just a young man faithful in prayer and willing to open the church doors. I was still wrestling within myself about my own calling, unsure if I was best suited for the pulpit or some other type of public service. But that morning I knew that God was calling me to teach and preach the gospel. I didn't think it would ever be my sole full-time vocation, but I was certain I was destined to be a preacher and not a politician.

The chapel was empty and I was alone with the Lord. I stepped behind the glass lectern and said to Him, "If You really want me to preach, it's okay with me. Just help me to be a good husband and a great father to my children, and I will serve You till You call me home." It was not a long prayer, but I meant it. It is a day that, after a quarter century, I still remember because it was the day I buried my own giant's head. It was the day I set "dream goals" for my future as I began to ask God to allow me to pastor a church filled with thousands of people of different generations and nationalities and colors. I asked Him to allow me to travel and preach around the world and see people come to know Christ on a global scale. I asked Him to allow me to write books and train leaders. I asked Him to allow me to mentor preachers, business leaders, athletes, and politicians around the world. It really was an impossible prayer and one I would dare to pray aloud only when no one was listening. The church leadership would have thought my prayer presumptuous and that I was getting way ahead of myself. But in the silence of the chapel, in the darkness before the dawn, with my hands still buried deep in my jacket pockets, I prayed aloud.

I believed that if God could protect my life from all the giants I had endured and overcome to that point, this dream I had been nurturing for more than a year was possible. I had confidence even though I hadn't had the courage to say it out loud to another soul and not even in prayer until that snowy day. I knew that God was able because of all the things He had accomplished in my life.

I buried the heads of the giants I had defeated in my past firmly in the soil of my future and determined to work toward that goal. I didn't know that twenty-five years later my prayer would become a reality, but I had a feeling it would. That morning after the older congregants arrived, I pulled out my blue journal and began to complete the outline of my church. I constructed the flowchart and began in my own rudimentary way to describe the ministries the church would perform in the community. I even wrote in the names of people I thought would be perfectly suited to fill positions. I never intended for them to actually work with me, but I used them as a template for the type of person I would want in those roles. I had no idea that twenty years later, three of the people I penciled in that morning would be serving with me in our church in Denver, in the very positions I outlined that morning.

I did not at that time have a name for the church, and I did not know where it would be. But I trusted that if I was faithful to the Lord and continued to do His will, He would bring me to the Jerusalem of my own dreams—to the city of my personal promise. I believed that then for me, and I believe that now for you.

5

RETURN TO GIBEAH

The City of Re-Equipping

After defeating Goliath, David was thrust into the realm of King Saul, not as a visitor on loan from his father but compelled by Saul to be part of the culture and the court at Gibeah. He was not there for a temporary experience; he was now part of the system of rule established by God to occupy the region. He moved into territory ruled by the tribe of Benjamin and no longer lived under the dominion of the tribe of Judah.

Even though David was not in a strange nation or surrounded by foreign people, he had to adjust to a different culture. He had to immerse himself in this new world and needed re-equipping. Just as an army has to step back to regroup and re-arm after a major battle, David had to do the same. In Gibeah, David discovered he was to be re-equipped with a new role, purpose, and destination. All of those were part of an important transitional time essential for the cities to come, and David had to be in Saul's court to receive them.

Equipped with a New Role

After David defeated Goliath, King Saul asked Abner, "Whose son is this youth?" (1 Sam. 17:55). Saul supposed that Abner, captain of his army, would know whose son he was, especially because David fought so valiantly. But Abner had no idea, because David was not in the army.

King Saul didn't recognize David, whom he had expressly summoned from the barley fields of Bethlehem to sing to him, even though we would expect the king to recognize the boy who'd brought him such peace. However, have you ever run into a coworker at a shopping mall and not recognized him or her? Have you seen a college friend at a concert and not realized who the person was? It is common to see people out of context—out of the roles you are accustomed to seeing them in—and not be able to place them.

In addition, as you grow up, it can be difficult for your siblings and parents to envision you as an adult with a job and a family. They may find it hard to stop treating you as a child. That is why the Bible says that "no prophet is accepted in his own country" (Luke 4:24). But we are not frozen in one role or area of life; we are constantly evolving and becoming who God wants us to be. The transitions of our lives can be so dramatic or rapid that people might get stuck seeing us in the ways they are accustomed, even though God has transitioned us to new roles.

Our identities won't change, but the roles we play in advancing the purpose of God change all the time. David was still David, but his role of service changed, and that rapid change prevented Saul from being able to identify him. You have to be prepared for the possibility that you won't be recognized by people who knew you in a previous role. Be careful not to fault people for this error; it is the work of God. The heavenly Father never asks your peers for permission to promote you. He does His sovereign will, and this often leaves others grasping for the "old you" when God has already created a "new you" in a new role.

Kyle Speller serves as one of the associate pastors at our church in Denver. He stands an impressive six foot six and is a gentle giant. He has such a soothing baritone voice that he has a side business emceeing special events around the country and doing voice-overs for radio and television commercials. If you ever get to see the Denver Nuggets play at the Pepsi Center, the announcer you hear calling the action from courtside will probably be Pastor Speller. His heart is so big that people come to him from all walks of life. He is a warm and friendly pastor, and that is why I wanted him on our team at The Potter's House of Denver.

Pastor Speller is also one of the coaches for the basketball team my thirteen-year-old son, Jonathon, plays on. And although I can firmly attest that he coaches with the same Christian principles that guide him as a pastor, his smooth and easygoing manner is left in the locker room. When he puts that whistle around his neck, he becomes another man.

I love to attend Jonathon's basketball practices because I love to watch him play, but I equally enjoy watching my humble and mild-mannered associate pastor become the wild and motivating coach who drives his teams to victory. It is worth the price of admission to see the cool pastor yell out a play with that booming voice, wildly gesticulate as a referee misses an obvious call, and roar out the command "Hands up!" To watch him run a practice with the efficiency of a marine sergeant makes me giggle inside, because I have seen this man take crying newborns in his arms at their christenings and soothe them to sleep with his calming voice. He is the same person at heart, but the equipment needed for his coaching role is radically different from what he needs to pray with people around the altar. He is the same man, just with different equipment.

As God transitions you from city to city, be prepared for people to ask, "Who are you?" In fact, you might ask yourself the same question. God will empower you to walk in a new dimension of grace so rapidly that you hardly recognize yourself. Don't question the transition and don't second-guess His decision for your life. Your identity has not changed, but your role has been redefined.

EQUIPPED WITH NEW ALLIES

Jonathan, the son of King Saul, saw and noticed David when he returned from battle. We cannot be sure if the two had encountered each other before when David was singing in the king's court, but we know that this time Jonathan took full notice. It is as if the felling of the giant removed blinders from all eyes and people finally saw David for the champion he had always been. As soon as David presented himself in court, Jonathan saw David, and their two souls became "knit" together: "It came to pass, when he had made an end of speaking unto Saul, that the soul of Jonathan was knit with the soul of David, and Jonathan loved him as his own soul" (1 Sam. 18:1).

When the Bible speaks of the soul here, it uses the word *nephesh*, which comes from the word for *breath* in Hebrew. The Bible describes the friendship of David and Jonathan as if their breaths were knit or tied together. David and Jonathan had such a vital connection and friendship that one could barely tell where one person began and the other ended. It was not the bond of a sexual couple, in which the physical act creates the bond; their bond needed no physical act to cement it because it was instantly built in the soul as if their two lives were connected to the same source.

As soon as David reintroduced himself to Jonathan's father, this odd couple formed an immediate bond. One was from the big city and one from the fields, one from Judah and one from Benjamin, one the son of a king and the other the son of a herdsman. But both were valiant and brave. These two men were so akin to each other in soul—both great warriors born for battle—they seemed cut from the same cloth and truly brothers. Finally, David had found a brother who would never be jealous of him, would never desire his place, and was willing to share his glory.

In the Pacific Islands, there are many cultures that have incorporated into their greeting the "sharing of breath." They will lean their foreheads together and breathe in the same air at the same moment. With this primitive and primal gesture, they instantly launch a friendship that transcends death. The covenant bond between David and Jonathan was of so much benefit to David that even after Jonathan's death, David inquired if there was some person in his line whom he could bless to honor their covenant.

Gibeah was a city where David forged covenants and discovered relationships that redefined him at the next level. The level of friendship and mentorship David received from Jonathan was so valuable to him that the two became inseparable. Only death would separate them, and even Jonathan's blood tie to his father was not strong enough to break the soul tie he had with David. Imagine how restorative this relationship was for David, who from all scriptural accounts had a strained relationship with his brothers. He never really experienced the camaraderie and closeness that brothers in a normal relationship can experience, compounded by the fact that his brothers were rejected by God as possible future kings. This certainly would have been more than enough to create tension among siblings.

Jonathan became the first friend of David the Scriptures show us. Jonathan did not treat David as inferior, for this was not the nature of their covenant. Jonathan gave David his princely garments so he would be dressed correctly at court. He girded him with his own girdle like a big brother teaching his younger brother how to wear his clothes (18:4).

God might give you a fellow warrior who finds breath in the same places that you breathe—someone you can show your weaknesses to, someone who will mentor you not as a professor does a student but as a brother. When your city changes, your relationships also must change. This is critical to making it in this new city of your life. It is not that the old friendships, familiar and comfortable, are now null and void. In fact, later on we will see David's brothers rally in support of him when he must hide out in the cave of Adullam (1 Sam. 22). But new relationships come into play in our lives without replacing the others. God knows that you have to embrace new relationships to equip you to be sustained on this new level. In His grace, He has prepared people who do not have to wrestle with a previous impression of you and can step in to support you in your new role.

As God sends these new relationships into your life, you have to be open to receiving them. When you have been rejected and abused by others in your past, it can be hard to open your heart to new people, but this is critical to understanding the new stage of life you are in. You cannot drag your past pain into your present. You cannot allow the ghosts of your past to haunt your future. The path to your future can be hindered by seeing new people through the lens of yesterday's relationships. Moving forward requires stepping into new relationships, and there is no progress without making those emotional adjustments. These people can stretch and challenge you to think and act in new ways. They will challenge you to adjust to your new city by learning the language and customs of this new place. God is requiring you to adopt a new mentality—a new normal—and only these relationships can help you understand it.

EQUIPPED WITH NEW TOOLS

In David's new city, there were also new skills he must master: new weapons and tools he had to become acquainted with quickly. His slingshot was permanently retired; we never again hear of him using this weapon. It was useful in one season of his life, but the type of warfare he would face from this point on changed. He would need to master the bow and sword and become comfortable wearing armor. These new weapons and the skill for wielding them were necessary in this new phase. We must be thankful for our old skills but also be adaptable enough to learn new ones. New cities require new abilities, and we must be willing to learn new things.

Living on the streets of Boston at such a young age changed me. I was only six years old, so I had to learn how to steal food from the grocery stores and hide in the dark. I spent most of my days at the Boston Public Library in Copley Square. I would hide among the musty stacks of old books and read the children's books from cover to cover. If I scraped together some money, I would go to the corner diner and pretend my mother had sent me to order her some food. I would act as though she were right outside, pay for it dutifully, and then retreat to the library, where I would pretend I was meeting my mother.

I was constantly acting as though I had an invisible parent—as if I had an adult watching over me from a distance, following me, or preceding me at all times. I would sneak into the library bathroom and wash my skinny body in the sinks. If I heard someone coming in, I would run to a stall and wait for him to leave. I did not want anyone to know that this little boy was all alone.

I learned how to detect footsteps. I learned how to sleep on rooftops. I learned how to make people believe I had a parent nearby when, in reality, I was very much alone. Of course, now I know that God was watching over me. He was the dutiful and diligent parent who protected me in the shadows of that terrifying time in my life. But in those days, I didn't really know it.

I prayed constantly, not with the polished words of a preacher but with the simple words of a lonely child. I started a continuous conversation with the Lord in those days of trouble that has continued even to this hour. I experienced the intimacy in prayer that is birthed only from the womb of adversity. But I also learned how to wake up out of a dead sleep and run like the wind. I learned how to read people quickly and discern what dangerous adults to avoid in the streets. I learned how to scramble in the streets for money and run errands for pocket change. I carried grocery bags at the Stop & Shop for nice old ladies who would give me tips. I told myself bedtime stories and sang praise songs as lullabies to survive the dark nights alone in Franklin Park.

These were the weapons and skills I needed to survive. I refused to go home or reach out to anyone who might know my mother. I loved my mother so much that I did not want her to get in trouble with the police, but I had decided I would never again go home. To me, being frightened in the streets was much better than being afraid in my own home. Making my bed in public parks, under balconies, and on school rooftops was horrible, but I learned to endure it. I had to develop the weapons and tactics that would allow me to make the streets my home, but they were rendered almost entirely irrelevant the moment I walked into the beautiful suburban home of my paternal aunt and uncle. I did not need to hustle for tips, steal food, or hide in the shadows. My aunt and uncle were not just financially stable; they were financially strong. Their home was spacious and well furnished, and they had more than enough food. In their home, my street skills and weapons were no longer needed. My prayers had been answered, and I was safe at last.

David faced a similar situation. His days of watching sheep alone were over. He would never again encounter a bear with his slingshot or grab a lion by its mane. He would be surrounded by men who would risk their lives to bring him a cup of cold water

(2 Sam. 23:16). His own nephew would fight off giants to keep him safe (21:17).

Jonathan became a strategic ally for the future king. He gave two of his personal weapons to David, changing the arsenal from that of shepherd boy to that of man of war. These were two different kinds of weapons: arrows for distance and a sword for close combat. These two weapons mirror two separate but important weapons in the arsenal of the believer: prayer and the Word.

The arrows represent the power of prayer. Through prayer, we can be a great distance away and still find our target. We can shoot down the attacks of the Enemy and throw the opposition into confusion. I can sit in my study in Denver and fire arrows at the Enemy waging war at a sister church in Melbourne, Australia. I can sit in my chapel in Denver and launch arrows on the Enemy attacking my friends all over the world. Through prayer, I can shoot arrows at the Enemy attacking my two sons. I can shoot into the future and reach into the past. I can break generational curses and decree blessings on unborn grandchildren. The arrow is a distance weapon that mostly meets a moving target. In the hands of a gifted archer, it is most deadly, and David developed his skill with this weapon well.

We also see the arrow as a metaphor for children and the future: arrows in the quiver. So we can see this gift-giving act by Jonathan as symbolically giving David his future; it represents the abdication of the future kingship that by right belonged to Jonathan. Perhaps Jonathan perceived that the kingdom was promised to David. It is possible that the openness of their relationship allowed David to disclose to Jonathan what Samuel had already decreed. Maybe Jonathan did not just see David as his brother but also acknowledged him as his future king.

In the city of Gibeah, David encountered someone who discerned who he would become. In your Gibeah, you will find similar people. They are not prophets like Samuel who declare the future but never prepare us for it; they are peers who begin to equip you for who you will become. Jonathan handed David his royal dynasty symbolically when he handed him his quiver and bow. Jonathan knew that David was not a rival for his throne but the true recipient, and until his death he demonstrated his love and fidelity to David, because their covenant was never broken.

Jonathan also gave David his sword, which, of course, is not a long-distance weapon. It is a weapon used in close quarters. One does not hurl a sword. It stays firmly in the hand of the soldier and is used to attack an enemy who is just arm's length away. The sword is made of forged metal, and it is honed to a razor-sharp edge. Throughout the Bible, the sword symbolizes the Word of God. In this, we can see that Jonathan symbolically gave David his personal word—his true covenant.

I pray that in your Gibeah, you will meet a Jonathan who will hand you his sword—that word of deliverance that will help you overcome you enemies. The bloody sword of Jonathan was a prize because it faced a garrison of Philistines. And true covenant relationships cause us to share the words that helped bring down the strongholds in our own lives—not the quick-fix statements and trite, formulaic pronouncements that pretend to be preaching but the bloody word of our personal testimony. These are the truest stories of God's grace in our lives.

I encourage people to share the word that saved their lives with those they are in close covenant with. I don't mean the neatly packaged testimony that can be shared in a nice sound bite; I mean the bloodied word of our own testimony. When you give others that word, you are giving them a weapon they can use to fight their own close-up battles. There are real battles we must face, and only those real words can become the swords in our hands with which we can fight.

Equipped with a New Perspective

One of the rewards David was supposed to get after killing the giant was the hand of the king's daughter in marriage. This was an important part of David's ascent to royalty because the marriage would be a clear alliance between the royal house of Benjamin and the house of Judah, thus paving his way easily to the unified throne of Israel. Saul intended to give to the champion his eldest daughter, Merab, but in an act of treachery decided not to deliver her to David and gave her to another man. Merab means "increase." Saul did not want David to increase and conspired for him to fall in battle. He sent David away from his men of war and made him a captain over one thousand soldiers. But this ploy backfired on Saul because the distance between the two of them allowed David to stand on his own and triumph.

When people shun you because they are intimidated by you, do not despair. God will use the separation to make it clear to everyone that He is on your side. Proximity can occlude your individual call. Saul should have kept David close so his accomplishments would have blended in with the victories of the king's mighty men. Instead, the separation meant David stood out even more. The isolation set David up for decoration, and people took notice of what God was doing in his life.

Merab was given to a man from the territory of Issachar. This reminds me of Laban, who gave his elder daughter, Leah, to Jacob instead of his younger daughter, Rachel, in payment for seven years of service (Gen. 29). Yet the inclusion of Leah in this love triangle, however painful, resulted in the birth of Judah. If there was no trickery on the part of Laban, there would have been no Judah, the son of the "wrong" wife.

Saul's trickery had much the same effect as Laban's, for the daughter he gave to David, Michal, ended up blessing David's life. She truly fell in love with him and defied her father to save David's life. What men mean for evil God will turn for your good, so do not be discouraged by treachery because God is keeping the records and will turn it for your good.

Michal's name means "streamlet," or "brook." This is beautiful symmetry because it was the stone David extracted from a brook that felled the giant, and it was that stone that saved his life. Perhaps what people think they are reducing you to is the very thing that will save your life. Do not despise their broken promises or their ill-treatment, because God can use the leftovers to get you over. He can use those people who are almost a gag gift to enrich your life. Saul would not give David his firstborn as was promised, but Michal loved David, and that provided a greater reward.

It is better to be in the company of people who truly love you than to be in the company of people who have a better "pedigree" or status. I would rather be in the presence of people who have an authentic and godly love for me than those who are compelled by self-serving interests, such as title or position or money. If people join with you because of some external factor, their loyalties will shift as circumstances shift. Michal loved David not because she was forced to but because she desired to. When Saul's heart turned murderous toward David, she was still on the warrior's side. This so-called "wrong" wife had the most value to David.

I encourage you to avoid people whose love must be purchased, prompted, or prodded. These people will not be with you when the tides turn in your life. God providentially purposed the second choice. Sometimes man's rejection is really God's protection in disguise.

EQUIPPED WITH A NEW PURPOSE

As King Saul heard the songs of the women of Israel, his heart turned evil toward David. Never had a single song created such danger or caused so many lives to be lost. Simply because the women sang that David killed more enemies than Saul, the king assumed that his soon-to-be son-in-law would stage a bloody coup and rip the kingdom from him physically, as the prophet Samuel had already done symbolically (1 Sam. 16:13).

King Saul decided to act. Though David had done nothing against him, Saul pinned him to a wall with his javelin. It was one of those times when Saul was under the influence of the evil spirit that tormented him (18:10–11). The Bible tells us that David was playing his harp, as he had done in the past, but this time the music could not soothe the savage beast driving Saul. When it is no longer your season to serve in one capacity, you cannot return to it. David was a minstrel before he slew Goliath, and that role worked for him in that season of his life. But even though he was in the same city and serving the same king plagued by the same evil spirit, the grace that was upon David had changed.

Be careful that you don't attempt to operate as if you are living in a past season when God has already promoted you. The tools and tactics of your past lose their effectiveness when you are publicly promoted, not because you are less anointed but because the people you have been willing to serve may be so blinded by their own jealousy that they can no longer receive your ministry.

When the people you intend to help perceive you as a threat, they become almost impossible to minister to. It would be years before anyone could convince Saul that David was not his enemy. At this point, blinded by his jealousy, Saul picked up his javelin and hurled it at David to pin his body to the wall of the court. He literally tried to nail him to the wall (foreshadowing Calvary). We can learn from David's conflict with Saul that when people reject your gifts, you shouldn't let it discourage you. Switch your focus and purpose. Switch from singing for that king to singing for the kingdom.

Disappointment can derail us, but we must not allow it to destroy our gifts. The next time we see David singing, it is before the ark of the covenant (2 Sam. 6), the literal throne of the shekinah glory of God. Don't allow people to steal your song; just find someone else who is worthy of it, which David did wholeheartedly. He never serenaded Saul again, but he would lead all of Israel in serenading God.

As painful as this must have been for David, this "pinned to the wall" experience was necessary for his development. In Gibeah, he learned that the only king he could trust was the Lord. Saul was his father-in-law and his earthly king, but David could trust only his heavenly King. This kind of experience is critical for the development of every great leader. In fact, I believe that a person who has not been disappointed by a leader is probably not qualified to lead. Jacob had to be cheated by his uncle Laban before his name could be changed to Israel. Joseph had to be imprisoned by Potiphar before he could be allowed to lead the food program for Egypt. Moses had to be persecuted by Pharaoh before he was qualified to lead the Israelites. The apostles of the early church first had to be persecuted by the high priest and king before they could spread the message of the gospel globally. There is definitely something good that comes from being disappointed, misused, and misunderstood by a person in authority. It makes you more sensitive to the people you are charged with leading because you remember how it felt to have a person in authority speak evil of the good intentions in your heart.

Learning where to place my trust was the primary lesson of my life before I was eight years old. I didn't learn it in a classroom, and no teacher instructed me in it. I learned it alone, sleeping on the hard streets of Boston. I learned to put all my trust in God. This is the truth that has carried me around the world and has anchored the skiff of my soul in the most tempestuous of seas. I trust God. Had my world not been shaken as it was, I might not have learned this lesson so early.

I can sing with David the pain-filled words of Psalm 27:10, for when both my father and mother forsook me, the Lord really did take me up. The Lord watched over me and comforted me, and this experience left me with a rock-solid confidence that has not wavered much, even when I have been tested since those days.

David could not trust his father, who seemingly forgot he even existed when the prophet came to call. He could not trust his jealous brothers, who treated him with contempt when he came to the battlefield. He could not trust his king and father-in-law. Every family member and authority figure had disappointed David, but even this worked toward his good. Gibeah is the place where we learn to trust God. The javelins thrown at our heads should cause us to fall to our knees. We must lean completely upon God, armed with a quiet confidence that comes from knowing He never fails us. In time, we become thankful for the walls, the javelins, and even the treachery because these pains have produced true power in us. The crucible of crisis has crystallized our character and fixed our faith in such a way that we can be thoroughly persuaded that God is on our side.

EQUIPPED WITH A NEW DESTINATION

As we can see, Gibeah was a city of many mixed emotions for David. He formed a covenant with his friend Jonathan and met his first wife. He was given the weapons of a warrior and became one of Saul's mighty men. He was promoted to captain of one thousand men and at a young age led men in battle. Gibeah was the place where the singer was sung about and his popularity surged.

In Gibeah, he was given access to the royal courts, not as a mere servant, but as son-in-law to the king. In some ways Gibeah was the best time of young David's life. He must have thought he was finally approaching the fulfillment of his personal prophecy.

Then, with the swiftness of a javelin thrown by a mighty arm, the whole situation turned around. Saul put him in harm's way, changed the bargain and demanded a second dowry for his daughter, and sent David off to die at the hands of the Philistines. Saul hoped his rival would be removed permanently without having to get his hands dirty. But even this plot failed, for David proved to be a skillful leader by defeating and killing two hundred Philistines. He then presented their foreskins to Saul as a double dowry for the hand of his daughter.

David handled himself wisely and never dishonored Saul. This caused the flame of his fame to burn brighter in Israel. Not only did he defeat Goliath but he also doubled the dowry and married the young princess. Imagine the songs that filled the streets as all of Israel watched his exploits. Saul was so angry and afraid for his kingdom that he abandoned all sense of civility. He sent his messengers of death to David's house with orders to kill him. Prince Jonathan had already informed David about his father's desire to assassinate him and had David hide out until he made Saul swear not to do it.

After David again defeated the Philistines, the evil spirit returned to Saul, who broke his word and sent messengers of murder to the house of David. This time Michal learned of her father's plot, and because she loved David, she lowered him from her window to escape into the night before the messengers came to kill him in his bed. When Saul's assassins discovered her subterfuge, they brought her before the king.

If David had been given Merab as promised, she might have given him up at the insistence of her father. Instead, Saul's treachery backfired, and Michal's love led her to defy her father and let her husband escape. It turned out that the "wrong" wife actually saved David's life.

I have learned that God always opens a window when we are up against those people or things that would keep us from our destinies. It might not always be a neat and easy escape. Sometimes God has to sneak you out. None of us likes to retreat into the night; we would rather overcome our enemies in a blaze of glory. But picture the brave champion of Israel, the valiant giant slayer, sneaking softly out of his wife's window, hoping not to be seen or heard. This image is as important for us as the one we have of David holding the severed head of Goliath in victory. Too often we want to win with style points, but David is teaching us that sometimes it is better just to survive.

To the physically abused woman, I say just leave and survive. Pack up your children and whatever else you can carry on your back and just get out of that situation. There is no need for a grand declaration of faith or a big confrontation with your abuser. Just slip out into the night and survive.

To the emotionally troubled or the addict, I say to just get help. Stop trying to cope with the problem by yourself and find a professional with whom you can sort through your issues. There is no cowardice in getting help. There is no lack of faith in seeking professional assistance. The goal is just to survive.

What if David had decided he was going to confront Saul's assassins head-on and had gone out the front door with no support? David entered Gibeah victoriously through the gates of the city, with the women of the city dancing and singing in the streets. But this entrance is juxtaposed by an inglorious exit. He snuck out of Gibeah without any fanfare.

David again could have used a narrator to tell him that this was not the end. Gibeah was not his last city, for he had so many more to encounter, and one day he would rule this city. David didn't take much more from this city than experience. He had no bread, no sword, and no position, but in Gibeah he discovered how to lead, love, learn, and lose.

Don't allow the things that have ended strangely in your life to make you believe you are at your end. You have many more cities to conquer and much more life to live, because as long as you have a promise from the Lord, even your strangest endings are not the end. God is using your Gibeah to re-equip you for the battles ahead. Don't confuse your college with your career. Gibeah is just the place to be re-equipped, and its abrupt ending is not a foreshadowing of the rest of your life; it is an indication that you have learned everything this city was designed to teach you and it's time for you to move on.

6

GATH

The City in Hell's Backyard

In the time of David, Gath was a Philistine-controlled city. David fled there to escape Saul but was discovered and captured by the Philistines. He had to pretend to be sick with madness in order to save his life. Some scholars have been critical of this behavior, believing deception to be unacceptable for a true biblical hero. They think David should have faced down the Philistine hoard again and asserted his faith in God. I understand their disappointment, but I also understand there are choices we make in life-or-death situations that require wits and wisdom in order to survive. David's pretending to be crazy to escape the deadly wrath of the king of Gath was probably the smartest play.

To comprehend this stage in David's life, we have to understand what he had just endured. Saul took everything from him. David could not return to Bethlehem and his father's house without endangering his family, so subsequently he was robbed of his friendship with Jonathan, his house, his wife, and all his possessions. David was a fugitive on the run without money, food, or support.

Just the day before, David had been captain of a thousand-man troop and was the esteemed son-in-law of the king. But within twenty-four hours, he was destitute and running from the very man he had served so well. At just twenty-four years of age, David was in a complete tailspin. He was not a mature man who had experienced rejection on this level before; he had just moved beyond the carefree ways of an adolescent to fighting a battle completely out of his depth. He was facing an enemy he could not fight with his bow, arrow, or sword. How does a bloodied warrior fight an adversary he is not allowed to kill? How would David justify the rapid fall of his fortune in light of the prophecies he received from Samuel about his royal future? Where was it safe for David to hide from Saul?

Remember that Samuel told God that if Saul knew why the prophet was going to Bethlehem, the king would put even him to death (1 Sam. 16:2). So David could not rest in the protection of Samuel, not without putting the prophet at risk again on his behalf. He could not hide anywhere in Israel without putting innocent people at risk. David had nowhere to run but into enemy territory, to a region where Saul had no dominion. He ran to a place where no innocents would be put in jeopardy for aiding him (21:1). He ran to Gath, the home of Goliath, which was also one of the five royal cities of the Philistines.

In his haste to escape, David retreated into this Philistine stronghold. Most likely, he was seeking a place where he could come up with a strategy to protect himself and his family. Some might say this was like jumping out of the frying pan into the fire. But as I've examined the Scriptures and looked at the lives of many people I have known,

I've seen that this is normal when God is developing leaders. He will sometimes hide them right in harm's way. It's as if He deliberately deposits His heroes in dangerous territory to further prepare them to rule in the area He has designed for them. Do not be dismayed or discouraged when God allows you to temporarily go from a bad situation into a worse situation. This is what He calls progress.

BUSTED

Before being gripped by depression, my mother had enrolled my sister and me in an excellent educational program. This program bused inner-city children to the elite schools in the suburbs. She would wake us up early, dress us warmly to fight off the northern chill, and walk us to our bus stops.

I spent my first-grade year at the Parker School in Lexington, Massachusetts, located about fourteen miles from the city. For me, going to Lexington was like going to another world. It was a quiet and historic New England town—a bedroom community of the bustling city of Boston. My mother had carefully selected clean, safe schools for us. I was a bright and happy boy and flourished in this environment, and although I was part of a racial minority, I never felt I was. I liked the green fields and open areas, and the teachers were kind and attentive. I really liked the school. But I missed my entire second-grade year, as this was when I had run away and was living on the streets. This perilous time in my life resembled David's brief season in the city of Gath.

As the summer turned to autumn and the leaves began to fall, it was getting too cold to spend my nights in Franklin Park or on the rooftop of the Jeremiah Burke High School behind my mother's apartment. I still had no thought of seeking out a family member or family friend because I really did not want my mother to get in any trouble. Spending most of my days in the Boston Public Library, I came in through different entrances and varied the times I spent in certain parts of the library so I would go unnoticed. But that was much easier to do in the summer when the library teemed with children. With the start of the school year, the number of school-aged kids at the library in the mornings diminished greatly, especially in the early mornings, when I liked to slide quietly under the metal turnstiles and make my way to the stacks for warmth and sleep.

There was just no hiding anymore and no blending in. I knew sooner or later someone would notice this small black kid in a little jacket and tattered backpack who showed up every day without a parent. I knew that someone would call the authorities, but I didn't have any other place to go. My mother had brought us to the library so often that it was like an extended home for me. I felt her embrace in its marble halls and somehow felt protected there, even though I was surrounded by strangers.

One day a lady walked up to me and asked where my mother was, right out of the blue. Without a thought, I took off running, but they had already called the police. I led them on a good chase, as by then I knew that library better than the back of my own hand. I ran down ornate stairways covered with expensive art and through stairwells that smelled of urine and street people. Both were so familiar to me that I almost escaped, but my legs were too short to outpace grown cops.

They caught me on the side steps of the library as I was heading across the street into the Green Line subway station. I was busted. The two police officers asked my name, but I would not tell them. They asked for my parents' names, but I would not tell them. I was not belligerent or violent, I just did not want my mother to get in trouble and I had no intention of going home. I sat calmly in their cruiser and answered their questions, except the most important ones.

The police officers were kind and persuasive, using all kinds of reverse psychology to try to get me to slip up, but I had been on the streets too long to fall for their tactics. By now my mind was quick and I had become adept at reading people. Even though most adults treated me like a little kid, I was streetwise and perceptive well beyond my years.

The police officers had to do something with me, so eventually they took me to Boston City Hospital. I went along peacefully because they were too big to fight off without my stick, and I figured I could escape when they weren't looking. I was disgusted with myself for getting caught.

Using the inherent magic of their police badges, the officers somehow managed to get me admitted into the children's ward without even knowing my name. The staff escorted me to an open room with a soft hospital bed and a television, and they told me to take my filthy clothes off. I washed up in a little bathroom using a travel-sized bar of soap, brushed my teeth with a real toothbrush, and examined my overgrown hair in the mirror.

In a few hours, the kitchen staff started to bring trays of warm food. I remember thinking I should have gotten busted sooner. I ate green Jell-O and drank icy orange juice from plastic cups as various adults—a psychologist and the occasional social worker—tried to convince me to tell them who I was. It seemed as if not having a name for me meant they didn't have a way to process me, but living in limbo temporarily was just fine with me. I would rest up there and plot my escape later.

The doctors and other experts were very smart, but I was having nothing of it. I finally had a bed, a television, and three square meals a day. Clean bluish-green hospital pajamas appeared like magic every day, and all I had to do was outthink a bunch of grown-ups. This was the life.

I played with the other kids in the ward. I sat up and watched TV with the sick children and read to the little ones. I was obedient and caused no trouble, and the days wound on so easily that I have no idea how long I was there. The other children cycled in and out, some getting examined and others going to surgery or to the intensive care unit. I just stayed in my little space.

One quiet day, I looked for my clothes, but they had been taken away. I guess the staff figured I could not run away in hospital pajamas and slippers. Employees would pay me a visit to play a game of checkers, trying to disarm me and then ply me for information. I got really good at board games and told them nothing. The social workers came and went and the doctors seemed to change, but I was still there. Children also came and went along with their families, and each day blended into the next.

One day I looked up and saw my grandfather, Ernest Hill Jr., walking into my hospital room. At five foot ten, he was not a tall man, but he was heroic to me. He had reddish-brown skin and wavy, slicked-back hair and weighed a trim 165 pounds. But his voice was so high pitched that when he raised it, everyone who heard it would smile. He had a laugh, smile, and personality that were so big he could light up a room like a neon sign. He dressed dapperly in fine suits and handmade shoes. People did whatever he told them to do. Even though he never passed the fourth grade, I came to see him as a mathematical genius and a natural leader of men. He never forgot a face, name, birthday, or personal detail.

Granddad sat down on the edge of the bed and quietly told me that today I was going home with him. He added, "The Lord gave me a dream and told me where you were." I am not sure if his story was true, as I saw the face of a nurse who looked familiar. When she'd come to work in the ward, I'd thought I recognized her as the daughter of an old woman in our little church. She did not visit the church often, but even then I had a gift for remembering faces, as my grandfather did. I suspected that she tipped off my father's family, who were well known in our neighborhood, and Granddad had come for me. But that's not what he told me that day. He said the Lord had sent him and it was time for me to come home.

My grandfather was by no means a saint. And to my knowledge, he didn't really become active in any church or practice his faith with regularity until I was in my late teens and he retired to Augusta, Georgia, where he had been raised. I do know that he always had deep respect for God. The story of his life is so fanciful that even if those still alive who knew him swore to its veracity on a stack of Bibles, few people would believe it. Suffice it to say, he was not an ordinary man. He was respected and adored by his family and friends, all of whom were fiercely loyal to him, but he was feared on the streets. His temperament was so mercurial that he was dangerous to cross. One moment he would be sitting on the porch working on a trigonometry problem from one of his son's college math books, and the next minute he would be rallying his troops looking for blood.

Granddad had an uncanny luck that made him one of the most successful gamblers of his time in the black community. He never really considered himself lucky; he thought himself blessed by God despite his illegal activity. He knew that the arc of his life was so impossible that only God could be sustaining him. From time to time, he claimed that God would give him a "tip"—information that no one could know—and these tips had led to his fortune and even saved his life many times. And this time, one of these tips had saved mine.

The orderlies produced my clothes from somewhere and my grandfather, holding my hand, walked me down winding hospital corridors and out to the parking lot. He directed me to his impossibly long money-green Lincoln and drove me to his home.

I don't know what he said to the hospital staff or authorities, but I was free—free with a court order, doctor's prescription, and social worker's supervision. I rolled down the electric windows of his car and tasted the air, finally feeling safe for the first time in many months. In less than fifteen minutes, we were home. The whole time I had been in the hospital, I had not been more than two miles away from my grandparents' front door.

HIDDEN IN HELL'S TERRITORY

Just as we see how the hand of God played out in David's bad-to-worse scenario, Joseph is another example of this truth. God promoted Joseph from the arid pit of murder to the chains of slavery in the house of Potiphar. Joseph's brothers hated him so much that they decided to kill him and tell their father he was ravaged by a wild beast. Then the brothers got a better idea and decided to seek financial profit from his disappearance rather than killing him outright. They threw him into a pit until they could sell him for twenty pieces of silver to migrant traders. These traders actually ended up taking Joseph to Egypt, where he was purchased as a slave by one of Pharaoh's officials (Gen. 37). Although this was a terrible fate, studying the life of Joseph from beginning to end reveals that he was safer in Egypt than in his home territory.

Joseph's life never really would be in jeopardy in Egypt. He actually was more protected in the house of his oppressor than in his own father's house. His brothers seethed with murderous hatred toward him and probably would have killed him had he stayed. The rejection of his brothers was actually the hand of God protecting him from their homicidal tendencies.

In a society as bloody as Egypt was at the time, Potiphar had Joseph imprisoned when his own wife accused Joseph of attempted rape. Few people talk about the leniency of Potiphar with these trumped-up charges against Joseph. The slave master did not know that his slave had been wrongly accused, yet he kept Joseph alive. Joseph's own brothers sought to kill him for the far lesser offense of being better liked by their father.

Sometimes God's purpose for your life will send you to the seemingly wrong place. Maybe you were laid off from a good job, but that layoff turned into a payoff because that loss caused you to start your own successful business. Perhaps you were rejected by a loved one and thought your heart would never heal, but as life progressed, you realized that God allowed the rejection to be the vehicle of your own freedom and emotional health. Only by being out of the relationship could you see that it was unhealthy and that a more compatible person would be better for you. It could be you were once part of a church relationship that became so toxic that you had to break away, but in doing so, you found a new place to worship, where you were nurtured in your faith far more than you could have been in the old place.

These painful promotions can definitely feel like hell's territory but are still promotions. God is the great recycler; He uses it all for your greater good (Rom. 8:28). View your trouble as a promotion, and change your own narrative. What you say about your situation is important. When people have told me about their negative experiences, I say, "Thank God He got you out of that!" Sometimes things have to end badly or else they would never truly end.

God's amazing grace can sustain us even when our situation seems to go from bad to worse. It's as if God camouflages you with more trouble, making it look so bad that your enemies will not continue seeking to destroy you. This is the case with Joseph's brothers, who never gave him a second thought after selling him. Thinking his fate was sealed in the hands of the

Midian traders, they wrote him off, expecting to never see him again. Boy, were they wrong.

In the life of Moses, we know that Pharaoh decided that all the male sons of the Israelites should be put to death. Jochebed, Moses's mother, decided to put him in a watertight basket and float him down the Nile River. The baby ended up in the hands of the daughter of the man who had just signed his death warrant. Moses was cared for, educated, and raised at the table of his own would-be assassin (Exod. 2).

In the New Testament, evil King Herod ordered infanticide in Bethlehem to eradicate any hope for a rival to his throne. This time God used another dreamer—one who happened to have the name of Joseph as well—to carry the Christ child and his mother to safety in Egypt. This former place of bondage became their place of safety.

There, hidden from the attacks of Herod, Jesus was able to flourish. Jesus was safer in the company of strangers than in the company of His own kin. And hidden in foreign territory, the Savior of the world was saved (Matt. 2:13–18).

Your Enemy Knows Your Song

David ran to Gath thinking he could blend in with everyone else. He knew firsthand that Saul would use any means necessary to destroy him and his innocent family members. He was in Philistine country, and Saul dared not give chase there, so David assumed he could return to the anonymity he had before he killed the giant. Certainly, no one would recognize him. But

David had not realized the implications of his experience in his last city. Not only did the Philistines know his name but they also had heard his song.

God often uses your enemies to let you know you have arrived. Sometimes you don't even know you have reached the next city— the next stage of your development—until you discover that your enemies have already heard of you. David was so naive about his own fame that he thought he could go back to being unknown. He did not realize he had an international reputation and that the Philistines were describing him as royal. At times, our self-doubt blinds us and we need the outside perspective of our enemies to help us know we are progressing.

Recently, one of my friends who pastors a large and growing church came under the withering attack of a blogger. This nameless and faceless fraudulent Internet blogger set himself up as a committee of one and began to post falsehoods and outright lies about my friend. Those of us in ministry often have to deal with bloggers trying to gain "views" by posting libelous claptrap about us and our work.

I was upset by these unfair criticisms and called my friend to offer support. I was going to pray with him because most people in ministry are completely blindsided by these attacks. They are usually counseled to endure in silence rather than draw unnecessary attention to the lies by engaging their accuser. This is painful but prudent, because all these people typically want is for others to notice them. I expected this pastor to be sad, but he was elated.

"Chris," he said, "I finally made it! I am finally doing enough damage to the kingdom of darkness that the darkness has finally noticed I am here."

He felt that his enemies were the warning system indicating that his efforts to build the church—to feed and help people—were finally working. The Devil now had to use someone to fabricate lies. I called him to pray off sadness, but instead we ended up praising with gladness. The Enemy had told my friend he was in his next city.

How many times have you allowed people's jealousy to cause you to hide your light? How many times have you allowed people to tell you that you were conceited or proud, causing you to dumb down your abilities and gifts? Instead of allowing these caustic people to discourage you, let their words and deeds encourage you. You are firmly and publicly on the right track.

Not only did the Philistines know David on sight they also knew what the women of Israel and Judah had been singing about him. Likewise, sometimes people sing your praises to others and you don't even know it. Even though one person might want to harm you, it could be that a whole nation is singing your song. You can be so disheartened by individual rejection that you don't hear the sounds of those who recognize your steady successes.

BETWEEN TWO KINGS

David found himself in a grave dilemma because the courtiers of King Achish, ruler of Gath, discovered him and brought him to stand before their king. They recited the song and the exploits of David to him. At this point, David was afraid. The fear was so powerful that later, after his escape, he sat down and penned a psalm about the experience: "This poor man cried, and the LORD heard him, and saved him out of all his troubles. The angel of the

LORD encampeth round about them that fear him, and delivereth them" (Ps. 34:6–7).

The words of this song give us direct insight into David's mind in this situation. He was surrounded, isolated, and alone in the camp of his enemy. He was discovered by the king of Gath while on the run from the king of Israel. He was trapped between two kings. One king was too anointed for David to fight, and the other he was not yet strategically ready to fight. This represents the dilemma of being in an important and transformative state—when God has us hiding out in foreign territory and we cannot fight anyone.

There are "Sauls" we cannot fight even though they are fighting us. They are part of the family of God even if they are not acting like it; and starting a dogfight with them is not Christlike behavior. Instead, you have to honor them not for who they have become but for who they were. Saul had been demonized for the entire period David had personal contact with him, yet David would not use his influence with his tribe of Judah or the other tribes to launch a military coup against him, even though he had a legitimate reason for doing so. It is quite possible he could have produced an assassination of Saul due to his relationships with Jonathan and Michal. Doing so might have stabilized the kingdom. But David did not consider this, because he knew it would not honor his relationship with God. When dealing with Sauls, you have to remember that those who once were anointed and worthy in God's eyes are off-limits because you can't know His ultimate plan for them. It is better not to touch, fight, or even talk about God's anointed than to risk the catastrophic circumstances that come when you contend with them (Ps. 105:15).

Many times in recent years, my church members have asked me to publicly comment on the actions of pastors and leaders who are seen in the media. Each time, I have endeavored to keep my mouth shut, but not because I fear man and not because I don't have an opinion. When I was a young preacher, I let all my opinions be known. But as I have matured in my understanding of the Scriptures, I've realized that the sword of my words is not to be used on my fellow believers. I give leaders the benefit of the doubt and hold my own tongue. I don't want to bring the judgment of God upon my own head, as the Bible warns in Matthew 7:1. I have learned to be merciful, because one day I will need that mercy returned to me.

David would not kill Saul, believing he should honor him because the king was, at one time, anointed. Sowing seeds of dishonor only results in reaping dishonor in a person's own life. David knew this at a young age and would not fight Saul outright, instead choosing to live as a bandit on the run.

But David also was trapped by another king—Abimelech Achish, the king of Gath—who stood on the other side of him. This king represents the obstacle we face when we encounter enemies we should defeat but realize we are not yet ready. David was flat-out afraid of Achish, saying in Psalm 18:6, "In my distress I called upon the LORD, and cried unto my God." Some things are not to be fought in the season we are in, and Gath teaches us to be able to recognize when we're not ready. This is a valuable lesson, because many people have launched into Philistine territory prematurely only to discover adversity they were not strong enough to overcome. This is a tragedy, because being patient *now* would have yielded victory *later*. Although a "Goliath" can be felled individually, an "Achish" can be defeated only corporately. Kings exist in a system of dominion, so no matter how gifted we are as individuals, we cannot face them effectively until we have built, trained, and developed our own "armies." We have to know how to run a system to bring a system down. The individual can do great damage, but only a system of dominion can dismantle a system of dominion.

Samson, a supernaturally strong man and judge, did great damage to the lords of the Philistines in his time. But because the Philistines already had the means to perpetuate their system of leadership, the great blow Samson struck in his final act, though effective, was not a deathblow. The Philistines were still causing trouble for the Israelites long after Samson died. That's because an individual cannot conquer a kingdom; that kind of defeat requires an army. David could deal with Achish only once he had built a system—a unified army—that would be able to completely eradicate the enemy.

One of the meanings of the name Achish is "only a man." Too often we allow ourselves to be goaded into taking on battles with individuals instead of putting our energies into preparing teams to systemically solve the problem. King Achish was "only a man," and although David could kill him in Gath, David's time spent in one of the five Philistine royal cities gave him the insight to understand that killing one man—even one of their leaders—would not stop the Philistines.

HIDE YOUR ABILITY, NOT YOUR IDENTITY

David's time in Gath also allowed him to examine one of the Philistine courts from the inside. He saw the redundancy of leadership and how they arrayed their kingdom. They did not concentrate their leadership on one area or around one central king; instead, through alliance and communication, the five cities worked together to combat King Saul.

Their cities were strong and fortified, which they had been since the time of Joshua's invasion. Gath and two of the other royal cities still had the sons of Anak—the giants—in them. Their leadership was individualized yet interconnected. David had good reason to be scared, so he adopted an odd strategy: he acted insane. We have seen subterfuge in the Scriptures before. Both Abraham and Isaac told heathen kings that their beautiful wives were their sisters to try to avoid trouble (Gen. 20; 26). In Abraham's case, this was true because Sarah really was his sister, but he left out the part about her also being his wife. In Isaac's case, this was an outright lie; although Rebekah was his relative, they did not share any parents. Tamar dressed as a harlot and tricked Judah into sleeping with her, his own widowed daughter-in-law (Gen. 38). Rahab, the harlot of Jericho, lied to the messengers sent to her house from the king of Jericho to secure the safety and escape of the two spies (Josh. 2).

In all these instances, the Bible does not rebuke the individuals for their trickery. In fact, when the two patriarchs left the cities where they lied about their wives, they left with more riches than they had when they first arrived. The two matriarchs' lies were also rewarded, as they were both allowed to have children and raise their families in Israel. Even though the two sons of Tamar were sired as a result of her deceiving Judah into sleeping with her, he had previously lied to her, denying her his only living son after promising to replace the husband she lost. The Bible gives no scathing reprimand for her lies, and she, along with Rahab, would help make up the genealogy of King David.

I am not condoning their behavior, but I cannot join the chorus of biblical scholars who denounce them for outwitting people intending to rob them of their lives, livelihood, or futures. Samuel even engaged in deceit when he anointed David in secrecy as God instructed. God told Samuel to take a sacrificial cow with him to the household of Jesse so if Saul asked him what he was doing in Bethlehem, he could honestly say he was going to the city to offer a sacrifice.

Trickery when dealing with enemies or double-dealing people seems to be allowable, especially in the Old Testament, and David was by no means an exception to this rule. When King Achish's officials brought David to the Philistine king, "he changed his behaviour before them, and feigned himself mad in their hands" (1 Sam. 21:13). David started to act insane. He put on the performance of his life, even drooling on his beard. Some scholars suggest that he acted as if he were having an epileptic seizure, falling to the ground and foaming at the mouth. This Oscar-worthy performance caused Achish to be totally dismissive of David and ignore the warnings of his own officials. Achish could not see any threat coming from this man who looked like a lunatic, so he allowed David to escape, just as David intended.

When you are in a Gath situation in your life, it is okay to downplay your abilities, even though you cannot hide your identity. The experiences in your previous cities have likely rendered it impossible for you to hide your identity. But when you face an adversary you are not ready to fully confront, it is acceptable to give the impression that the "songs" they have heard sung about you are inflated. David could no longer hide his identity, but he could hide the fact that he was dangerous.

When you are dealing with an adversary better prepared to fight a battle than you are, it is wise to make that adversary believe that you are not a threat. Suppose you desire to move up in your company and have enrolled in classes to sharpen your skill set. In the course of moving toward a promotion, you might encounter some coworkers who do not want you to advance. In this case, you might want to keep quiet about the fact that you are working to improve yourself. Or let's say you have a contentious relative who is always competing with you, and you are in the process of buying another home. It might be wise to keep the peace by withholding that information, at least until the transaction is fully executed.

If David had not feigned illness, Achish quite possibly would have seen him as a threat and had him executed before David had a chance to raise his own army. It was more important to survive that day than to win style points in how he was going to do it. David survived, and although it was not as the shining hero, this picture gives us insight into the cunning nature of this future king. David knew it would be better to hide in plain sight.

In Gath, you learn not to show too much of your brilliance, for bright lights always hurt the eyes of people who have grown accustomed to the dark. You learn how to robe strength in weakness and how to govern your own tongue, assessing the strength of the enemy army while on their turf.

Gath means "winepress," and a winepress is where grapes are crushed to produce wine. Gath is so similar to Gethsemane, which means "the place of the winepress," that we should look closer. In Gath, David had to learn to be totally dependent upon God's sending angels to encamp around him and protect him from his enemies. David was crushed between the press of two kings, but from this experience flowed the sweet wine of the song he composed. In one of the verses David wrote, he said, "He keepeth all his bones: not one of them is broken" (Ps. 34:20). This verse seems to point us straight to Jesus, whose bones were never broken while on the cross. It was the custom with crucifixions to break the leg bones to help hasten the death. With Jesus, they did not do this, because He laid down His life; it was not taken from Him. He gave up His life precisely when He wanted to. He gave the Roman soldiers no reason to break His bones. This psalm David wrote became a messianic prophecy about Christ, our Savior, who also went through an ordeal in a place called "winepress." In the garden of Gethsemane, Jesus was in between two kings as well: His heavenly Father, who had asked Him to die as a sacrifice for our sins, and the kings of this world, who sought to torture and shame Him. Only His great love and steadfast obedience to the Father could stop Jesus from using His power to fight a physical battle.

The Son was so obedient to His Father's commands that there was no rebellion in Him, even though He despised the shame of the cross. Jesus prayed that the Father would allow the cup to pass from Him but was so submitted to the will of the Father that He surrendered His own will. Jesus had enough power to cause the entire battalion of soldiers arresting Him in the garden of Gethsemane to fall backward just by saying, "I am." But He did not use this amazing power to fend them off. He would not be goaded into a fight prematurely. Jesus, like David, refused to do battle before He was ready. According to the apostle Paul, Jesus played the ultimate trick on the princes of this world by getting them to crucify Him, because if they had known what it would accomplish, "they would not have crucified the Lord of glory" (1 Cor. 2:8).

Jesus feigned weakness to purchase real strength for us. In the winepress of Gethsemane, the sweet wine of our redemption was determined. As David wrote, "The LORD redeemeth the soul of his servants: and none of them that trust in him shall be desolate" (Ps. 34:22).

7

ADULLAM

The City of Leadership Development

Adullam is a city of great antiquity located in the hill country of Judah. Today the ruins of this city rest upon a hilltop that overlooks the valley of Elah, about two miles from the place where young David faced Goliath. Adullam is about thirteen miles west of David's birthplace of Bethlehem, so it is possible that he was already familiar with the area before he fled there to escape the hands of the Philistine king. But it is just as likely that David did not know the land and was simply led by the Holy Spirit to find refuge there for a season in his life.

It is amazing how God can lead you to a place of safety even when you do not know where you are going. Many times He will lead you to a new place of rest and strength so you can recover from the trauma of experiences you have just survived. For David, Adullam was such a place, where he could recover, regroup, and sort through the emotional upheaval that had struck his life.

Adullam has a history far older than the times of David, for it was one of the royal cities of the Canaanites at the time Joshua led the Israelite invasion. Even before the forty-year sojourn of the

Israelites in Egypt, the children of Abraham were familiar with the city of Adullam. Judah, the fourth son of Jacob and the fore-father of David, moved away from his father and brothers and settled in Adullam (Gen. 38:1). He found his first wife among the daughters of the Canaanites and raised his three sons. Adullam was a well-watered city and perfectly situated near a Canaanite trade route, which would one day become the Roman road that connected the city to the rest of the world.

Some five hundred feet high above the valley floor sits a flat-topped hill full of man-made caverns, some of which are large enough to accommodate several hundred men. It is this hill that most scholars believe housed the cave of Adullam, the fortress where David took refuge while on the run from King Saul. So when the Bible refers to it as a cave, it doesn't mean a cramped and closed-in space. It was not a dark or craggy hole. When visiting the ruins, one sees caverns with lofty ceilings that have been hewed out of the simple cave it might have once been. This cave now has ceremonial bathing areas and elaborate columns that support the ceilings. This is a fortress that sweat and blood have carved out of the rock of the hill. Many people worked countless hours to carve out a place to live in this rock, including the heavy work of carrying away discarded stones. David did not select a weak place to retreat to; he selected a hard place chiseled from the rock.

RECOVERY

David barely escaped King Achish, the Philistine king, and once again had to enter the kingdom of Saul. David's attempt to hide in enemy territory nearly cost him his life, so he had to risk returning to the dominion of Saul. But where does one hide from a king in the king's country? Knowing he could not return to his hometown of Bethlehem, he decided to go to Adullam to take advantage of the natural fortress that its caves would provide. It was here that David found time to sit and consider what had happened to him.

At times, the frenetic pace of our lives keeps us from doing any real reflection. Allowing stress and busyness to take over our lives is a huge mistake. We have to discipline ourselves to do the hard work of self-reflection and sort through the emotional pain that comes from having hard interactions with the people we love.

David was dealing with very painful emotions. No doubt he thought his days of living hard off the land were at an end after his victory over Goliath. He had traded sleeping in the sheepfold for the life of a soldier and the tents of the infantrymen. Battle had been no hardship to this brave warrior, especially knowing that once the battles were won, he would return to his warm house and the loving arms of his wife. David's life had been upgraded, and he thought he no longer would have to make a stone his pillow or sleep uncovered under the stars. But his life had spun out of control and been turned upside down. His comfortable bed in the palace of Saul and his secure position in the king's army were lost. It was over. David was sheltered in a cave, living off the land, and hiding out from the same king he had pledged to serve.

What do you do when the people you love won't allow you to love them, and your purest intentions are misconstrued as haughtiness and pride? David already had been misunderstood by his brothers and forgotten by his father. Now his father-in-law,

Saul, decided he was such a threat that he was determined to take David's life. This was the ultimate misunderstanding. Saul was detecting the hand of the Lord upon David, but he misunderstood that David would never use his favor with God to destroy Saul. He could not fight the people he loved. He would not kill his covenant friend, Jonathan, nor could he kill his father-in-law, so he had to run and hide. David's hands were tied because he had an adversary he could not attack. Facing opposition from his own family, he was immobilized by his own integrity and love, so he ran to the caves of Adullam to find his refuge.

This marks a painful time in the life of David because he was separated from his wife, Michal, and his friend Jonathan; neither would dare risk the wrath of their father to assist David any further. Despite the fact that both of them had covenant relationships with David, Saul disrespected these covenants and would not allow his children to honor them without forfeiting their lives. Saul was so enraged that he even threw his spear at Jonathan in a fit of rage over David (1 Sam. 20:33).

If Saul would kill Jonathan over his covenant relationship with David, how much more would he be willing to kill David's blood family? David knew that his family was also in jeopardy. No one who helped or harbored him would be safe, so David retreated to the fortress of Adullam to heal his emotional wounds and take stock. Even the mighty must take time out to recover.

Needing to rest and retreat doesn't mean you are a weak person; it is an indication that you are a strong person who has survived a tough fight. Just because your wounds aren't visible does not mean you are not wounded. I have learned that the most painful wounds are invisible to the naked eye. Rejection leaves no scar and requires no bandage, but it can leave a terrible wound. Left untreated, this wound can fester in one's soul. David was rejected by his family and his king, but he was not rejected by his God. True recovery begins when we realize that in spite of what we have been through and in spite of the level of rejection we have suffered, God has never rejected or walked away from us. It is His consistent love that brings about recovery. It is remembering the unfailing and unfaltering love of our Father that cleanses the toxic poison of rejection from our hearts. His divine acceptance heals us. The fact that He is with us and the power of His Holy Spirit is still leading us helps us find health and wholeness even in the caves of our lives.

BREAKDOWN IS BREAKTHROUGH

Because David swore to protect Saul and was in a covenant relationship with the heir to the throne, there was no way forward unless God made another way. David was checkmated by his own allegiances, so God had to overturn the chessboard of his life by allowing King Saul to attempt to kill David. Although David's personal life was in an uproar, he was free to move toward his prophesied destiny.

God often allows the life we've constructed to fall apart so He can put it back together His way. It is through the demolition of what we thought it should be that it becomes possible for what He intended to exist. God simply loves us too much to allow our love for the wrong people or the wrong positions to keep us in the wrong place. He is not satisfied with our own small schemes when they frustrate His higher and perfect will. God does not hesitate to shipwreck our plans when they are too small to carry the treasure He intends for us. He is not one to settle for second best when it comes to what He has in mind for His children. He takes out His hammer and starts breaking everything to bits, not with the haphazard hand of a child in a tantrum but with the skilled hand of a master craftsman.

David was not rejected at Adullam as far as God was concerned. To God, David was correctly positioned—purposely and deliberately placed outside the court of King Saul—because He was about to assemble the early and rudimentary configuration of David's own royal court. God began to teach him how to rule. Saul may have rejected him, but the land would not; it was promised to David and his tribe before Israel had crossed the Jordan. The land itself belonged to David, and there he would learn more about who he really was.

CARVED OUT

Inside the cave of Adullam are caverns shaped by people who desperately needed a safe and fortified place to dwell. There are wide walls and tall hand-carved ceilings so high that one man could easily stand upon the shoulders of another man and still not reach the top. This is not a place easily given to comfort; it is a place people had to forcefully claim for themselves with simple tools and backbreaking work. This cave was excavated by the careful hands of men who realized they had to carve it out to make it habitable for their own use. This is the same process God does with us in our own Adullams. He cuts out what He needs to remove so He can dwell within us. He excavates us to make us habitable for His presence.

God does not inhabit spaces He has not already touched. The excavated places are the places where He dwells. He increases our capacity for Him not with what He gives us but with what He cuts away. The carving process God puts us through is as much a transformation process as what was done in the cave of Adullam. He makes us more habitable—more easily accessible to His presence yet still fortified against the attack of the Enemy. When He enters our lives, He changes us from a dark and dirty place of no use into a place where He can dwell. He makes us a fortress where others can find shelter and escape. He makes us a place of instruction for those who lack knowledge and a place of encouragement for those who are afraid. The cave of Adullam is not just the place David escaped to; it gives us a picture of what God was doing in David's life. He was excavating David's life, making him into a fortress not just for himself but for the benefit of others as well.

Broken Family

In the cave of Adullam, a reunion occurred. When David made his escape there, somehow word got to his family and they decided to find him. It is interesting that they did not accompany him to the palace of Saul, nor did they join his cohort of troops when he was the captain of Saul's army. But now that he was destitute, alone, and the sworn enemy of a demonized king, they were compelled to meet with him. Even his brothers—including his oldest, Eliab—came to him in the cave of Adullam.

This breakdown in David's life produced another breakthrough because the strained sibling relationships were healed in the cave. The crisis due to Saul's threats caused the entire family to rally together. Sometimes trouble is a unifying force for families. When the level of difficulty we face becomes truly lethal, old disagreements and misunderstandings become insignificant.

I have seen families argue over who would get possession of an old, rusted-out pickup truck, outdated furniture, pictures with no significant value, and houses not one of them wanted to live in. I have seen sibling rivalries left over from childhood linger like dark shadows in adulthood. I have seen families come to blows over costume jewelry and even fall out over what song to play at a funeral. Having conducted many funerals, I've seen people at their lowest times, with emotions exposed like raw nerves. I've stood with people in these moments when they were at their best and their worst, sometimes making that shift from one moment to the next.

These people might fight, but the fire of their emotions is usually not hard to extinguish. After twenty years of doing all kinds of family interventions, I have learned how to walk into the fray and speak peace. I remind family members that they are the only survivors in the "family lifeboat." They are the sole survivors of a great storm—a storm that has taken from them someone they all desperately loved. I remind them that in the obituary, the deceased is always said to be "survived by" his or her family members. I encourage them to take their eyes off the pain of their great loss and look at who they have left. They are the survivors, and they will need each other more than ever to make it through the shipwreck of their pain. I have learned that if the family can unite around the crisis instead of hurling insults, past actions can be forgiven and reconciliation can begin even in the most broken families.

David's family did not blame him for bringing the ire of Saul upon them. They did not scatter to different places or escape on their own. They didn't look for their own private retreats to wait out the onslaught this murderous king was planning for David's family. No, they left their farms, homes, and possessions and came to David.

David was not the eldest brother, nor was he the titular head of the household of Jesse; in fact, he was the youngest and the least among them. Eliab despised his youngest brother, accusing him of being arrogant and evil (1 Sam. 17:28). He could not yet see who David was, even though he knew that David had been anointed by Samuel to be the king. But later, Eliab was quick to rally to the side of the youngest when it looked as though David were losing. The love David's family really had for him was demonstrated at Adullam—not because the brothers were *forced* to come to him but because they *chose* to.

For David and for us, hard situations have a way of revealing who is really on our side. Many people will rally to our cause when we are winning, popular, and rich, but we should mark carefully the people who rally to us when we're outnumbered and out-gunned. These people become like our closest family, because their faithfulness has been proven by struggle. God can use struggle to heal our broken families if we are willing to yield to His will.

In Joseph's case, his brothers would not have come to Egypt to purchase food if there had been no famine in the land. In their case, it was not their love for Joseph that drew them to Egypt but rather the food crisis. They had no idea Joseph was there, but we see that crisis united the family and through crisis they discovered that they could establish a relationship based on forgiveness and love.

The broken relationships of our lives can be healed. Sometimes this healing does not come through a hard confrontation but as a result of strong crisis. God allows things to happen that eclipse the trivial issues separating loved ones and help us realize that our need for each other is stronger than the pride that divides us. This was the case with David's family. Saul was bloodthirsty; he had a priest put to death just because he unwittingly fed and armed David, even though David had deceived the priest by saying he was on assignment for Saul. If Saul would allow an innocent priest to be killed, how much more would he unleash his demonic fury upon the family of David? David's entire family was in danger, and this danger drove the family together.

With the threat of Saul's army dangling like the sword of Damocles over all their heads, no one was asking David who his mother was or why he didn't quite look like his brothers. No one was trying to get him to return to watching the sheep or calling him prideful or haughty. David's brothers and all his father's family came to him to give him the comfort of family and also to crown him as their leader. David's family finally realized that Samuel's prophecy was coming to pass (1 Sam. 22).

It must have been one of the greatest moments of David's life when he saw his brothers and extended family coming to his cave.

They had the option of finding sanctuary in other places. David's father, Jesse, was the grandson of Ruth the Moabitess, so any one of his family members could have gone into Moab and found safety. Instead, they chose to stay in perilous Israel and take a desperate stand with David. This family vote of confidence was probably the encouragement David needed as he was discovering who he was in the cave of Adullam.

When your own family begins to see and acknowledge there is a divine call on your life, this is a turning point. When they say they can see that you are destined to do something specific and important—especially when they have misunderstood and misused you in the past—it is a powerful family embrace. We can only imagine how healing this was for David.

I have had people I loved deeply misuse and abuse me because they did not discern or accept my true purpose, but I also have seen God order the situations of their lives so they had to come to me later for help and forgiveness. Vindication is not vengeance, and it is better to be vindicated by the Lord than to take vengeance on people you really love. Being seen in the right light by your peer group is one thing, but to finally be recognized by your family gives you a level of closure and healing that is hard to describe. In Adullam, this happened to David, and I pray it also happens to you.

BROKEN MEN

David's family met him at Adullam, but they were not the only people who flocked to him in this fortress. The Bible says, "Every one that was in distress, and every one that was in debt, and every one that was discontented, gathered themselves unto him [in the cave of Adullam]; and he became a captain over them" (v. 2). These broken men were drawn to David because they had no reason to stay where they were.

We often unnecessarily spend years loitering in places of loss, stuck in situations that stifle our growth and have little potential to change. But we stay in them because we cling to the familiarity, even when the situation is so destructive that we should leave. I applaud the men who sought out David because they recognized they were broken and did something about it. They did not dig their heels in and say, "Well, this must be God's will for my life." When they heard that David was in the fortress, they went to him.

These men were in distress, in debt, and discontented. No doubt others in Judah and Israel were in similar situations, but these men were experiencing these things at the same time. They were desperate for change and looking for a chance, and when desperate, one will follow his or her savior even to a cave. These men had nothing to lose, so taking a risk on this outlaw David sounded like a good bet to them.

I love working with people who are sick and tired of being sick and tired. I have always taken calculated risks, so I identify with risk takers who have realized that the system they are in is broken. They have nothing to lose if they consider other options. I love to pray with people who are no longer trying to dictate to God how He should orchestrate their deliverance. They pray desperate prayers that fully give their Savior permission to save them any way He can. They are like the men who came to the cave of Adullam, and it is these men David guided until they became mighty.

LEVELS OF BROKENNESS

The Bible says these men were broken in three ways, and these three criteria will teach us the building blocks of the mighty.

Distress. The Hebrew word for distress, *matsoq*, comes from the concept of being in a narrow place. It comes from a root word that means "to compress." This is a powerful picture because these men felt they were living their lives in narrow, tight, and compressed places. When trapped in a situation and powerless to break out, the psychological restrictions seem more claustrophobic than even physical confinement. Living in the confines of someone else's decisions, designs, or dictates leads to a distressed life.

We are born to live not in the narrows of life but in the open areas. I want to be clear, though: walking on the narrow way morally does not mean living a narrow life (Matt. 7:14). We don't have to be narrow minded to live lives acceptable to God. Jesus lived a sinless life in the world, but He was the picture of a happy, loving, and embracing person. He was not limited by the minutiae of the laws of men nor the narrows of other people's opinions. The Pharisees of His day lived under His constant criticism because they embraced a harsh idea of morality but did not embrace people. He called them whitewashed tombs because they had polished exteriors and dead hearts (23:27). Jesus was free to love, think, and speak without the restrictions of the Pharisaical teachings and traditions, and it is this freedom our Lord desires for us all to experience.

Debt. Anyone who has owed something to someone knows that being in any kind of debt is a lousy feeling. The thinking that frames the Hebrew word *nasha* is to have debt imposed upon you with interest. This word can also be interpreted as "usurer," which today is the practice of making unethical or immoral monetary loans that unfairly enrich the lender. The Bible taught against charging interest on loans given to fellow Israelites (Exod. 22:26–27; Lev. 25:36–37). These people lived under financial domination from which they could not break free. They were trapped in unbiblical and unethical terms that made it impossible to ever become financially free. Imagine being forced into a debt you did not want to incur and then also being forced to pay interest. It is one thing to go into debt with the bank to purchase a house or a car, but it would be another thing to be forced into a loan to buy a house or car you did not want. To watch the interest grow and compound on the bill for something you did not even want would become daily torture.

Now you understand why these men were willing to throw off the chains of this financial bondage and join David in the cave. When you are feeling like a hamster perpetually running in the wheel of your financial life, you can feel as though your days are without meaning. You work and work, but the debt is not decreased. You save and pay and work all the more, but still the principal is untouched by your efforts. David did not welcome deadbeats who were merely walking away from their financial obligations; he welcomed the financially oppressed. He became their captain and offered them a fresh start, even if that start began in the chambers of a cave.

Discontentment. This word in the Hebrew, *nephesh*, deals not with the body or money but with the soul. The concept does not deal with a tangible issue that can be quantified easily or categorized neatly on a spreadsheet, and it cannot be easily described to someone else. The meaning is far more than the feeling we get when we feel limited by life, circumstance, or schedule. It is when the soul itself is under attack—when we feel a bitterness of the soul. This to me is the worst level of brokenness. Money can be replaced and narrow places can be escaped, but having bitterness in the soul can bring about a feeling of utter hopelessness. Soul sickness is worse than physical sickness because it robs us of the joy of being well. Being bitter in the soul is not something a medical doctor can just write a prescription for; there are no pills to heal the soul.

These discontented men knew there was something about being with David that brought healing to their souls. David's anointing, the destiny, the leadership caused these broken men to move toward wholeness. These broken men came to David even though it seemed he had nothing to offer them. But there was something intangible and almost indescribable about David that brought healing to their discontented souls.

There is an anointing that heals the embittered soul. There is a power found only in Jesus Christ, son of David, that causes people who are broken in deep places to find life and health. When Jesus touches our lives in this way, we cannot help but tell other people about it. Even if we can't explain it to them fully, they can see the joy and peace that come from being in the presence of our Lord. Once He touches our lives, we are willing to follow Him anywhere, even into the discomfort of a physical situation, because it is preferable to the discomfort we had in our souls before. This is why we call Him Healer: He heals us from the wounds that others cannot see.

HOMELESS AGAIN

I remember so vividly being brought to my grandparents' home.
It was like going to a family reunion. First, my older sister, Marie,
was there waiting for me to find my way to their door. She was
tall and smiling and happy to see me. She ran down the stairs and
embraced me. My paternal aunt and uncle also were there, and
they had with them my youngest cousin, Miles. They all wrapped
their arms around me and welcomed me home. When you have
lived without a place to rest your head and gone that long without
knowing if you would eat each night, being taken into any place
you could call home is almost magical. I felt as though the night-
mare of my life had finally ended. Then my grandmother came out
the front door, and I knew I was safe. She had a smile so bright it
made the sun look pale, and when her fat arms wrapped around
me, I knew that everything would be okay.

My grandfather held my hand, but it felt as though my grandmother were holding my heart. He was stern and rock solid and
provided a certain kind of protection for me just by his touch, but
she was honey-sweet and as a warm as a stoked fireplace on a cold
winter's night. Grandma Videlia caused my heart to melt, and I fell
into her arms and allowed myself to cry aloud. For months I had
cried silently, not wanting anyone to know I was alone. But with
her, I felt free to be a child again. I was home. The night was over,
and I was saved.

My aunt and uncle decided to take me in. They lived outside the city in a split-level house in the suburbs. They were both
professionals: he a bank vice president and she a highly placed

manager of one of the largest insurance companies in the city. Her office was on the upper floors of a skyscraper that dominated the horizon of our city. To me, they were rich, educated, and settled, and they invited me into their home. They had only one child, and their house had empty bedrooms. Their refrigerator was always stocked with food. They bought me a closetful of new clothes that fit me perfectly and got me the name-brand sneakers I had seen only on TV. The house was neat and well furnished with color televisions in every room.

On Friday nights, we would melt cheese in the fireplace and dip bread and meats in the sauce. They had toys for me to play with and a backyard with its very own playground set. My aunt and uncle were avid golfers, as were most of the people in my father's family, so they bought me my own little putter. They took me and my cousin to the golf course, and we would ride the cart across the manicured links. I spent endless hours exploring the woods behind their house and ended each day sitting on the swing set in the backyard, imagining I could fly. I thanked God every day that I was safe at last. I felt a million miles away from the urine-soaked alleys of the inner city. I thought I had died and gone to heaven.

My aunt and uncle had me tested for school and somehow managed to get me enrolled in the third grade even though I had never gone to second grade. My reading and math scores were sufficient for me to join my class at John Quincy Adams in Holliston, Massachusetts. I would carry my Incredible Hulk lunch box into the perfect suburban school, knowing it contained a healthy sandwich and all the snacks my aunt let me pick out from the supermarket. I was probably the only black boy in the third grade, but I didn't even notice or care. I was in school and I was learning. I was a normal kid who had survived an abnormal situation. I had a home.

I could imagine myself going to college and maybe even growing up to become a professional like my uncle. I liked to listen to my aunt and uncle's conversations while I ate my cereal and they drank their coffee and read the newspaper. I realize now that they were not rich people; they were upwardly mobile but firmly grounded in the black middle class. When they moved into that little town, prejudiced people had thrown rocks through their windows to try to chase them out of their small piece of the American dream. My aunt and uncle were hardworking people, but they knew how to laugh. They warmly embraced the responsibility of raising and educating the son of a family member.

My sister stayed in the city with my grandparents, so the entire family had joined in to care for the children of their deadbeat brother and son. Marie and I talked on the phone every night. We worked out a signal in which she would call and let the phone ring twice, and then I would call her back because the long-distance rates were cheaper from my aunt and uncle's house. Marie would tell me about her day at school and what she was learning, and we would marvel that we both were lucky enough to have made it to safe places. Most weekends my auntie would drive us to the city and we would all stay over at my grandparents' house. My other cousins would come from Maine and we would join with the family members who lived on the first floor of my grandparents' triple-decker and play on the street until the streetlights came on.

My grandfather would make me multilevel sandwiches with all kinds of meat and sweet pickles and cheeses. We would sit in their living room and watch golf and football games until night came and I fell asleep in a soft upholstered chair in front of their floor-model TV. I thought life could get no better. But one day it all got much worse.

A social worker came to my grandparents' house in the city and said that my sister and I had to leave. My mother wanted us back and had gone through the court system to bring us home. But in the meantime, the authorities didn't think it was right for my sister and me to be separated, so we were to be placed together in a foster home. We were taken from our family to live with strangers.

My grandparents and my aunt and uncle tried to fight the decision, but the rights of a biological parent prevailed. My cousin Miles and I would sneak down the stairs when we were supposed to be sleeping to eavesdrop on the adults discussing what they should do. They were all incensed because they had not even asked the government for one red cent to help take care of our needs. But the system had spoken louder than the voice of common sense, so we had to pack a little suitcase and go into foster care. I looked out the back window of the social worker's car as we drove away from our grandparents' home.

This time I made sure I knew how to get to my grandparents' house, as I intended to return the next day to retrieve the wooden stick I had hidden under their back porch. I had hoped I would never need that stick again, but when the talk of being returned to my mother's house was whispered among the adults, I had the feeling I would once again need my weapon. This time I marked

every street sign and every turn the social worker's car made so I
could retrace my steps.

My family was powerless to help me, my mother was not to
be trusted, and my older sister was falling apart in the front seat,
crying so hard she could hardly catch her breath. I was on my own.
I had to fend for myself. I would not grant myself the "weakness"
of crying. I just put on a brave smile and tried to memorize the
path back to get my stick. I felt homeless again.

I prayed the quiet prayer of a child. I still believed in the God
who had protected me in the dark of the night, the God who had
kept me from getting sick while I was living outdoors, the God
who had not allowed me to starve when I was eating out of the
garbage bins in the back alleys. I prayed that He would protect
me, because the adults were powerless to do so. The social worker,
the lawyers, and the judge were now in control of my destiny. But
I believed that ultimately my life was in the hands of the Lord.
At this time I was around seven or eight years old, but my faith
in God was battle tested and mature. I believed that He would
protect my life then, and I still believe that now.

INVISIBLE FORTRESS

The path of my young life, as I was living it, was so dark to me. I
felt powerless and totally unprotected by men. I loved my mother,
but I did not trust her. Even my rich and influential family members could not protect me from the rule of the government. I had
no idea where I was going or who I would be forced to live with,
but I still believed in God. In hindsight, I am thankful I was taken

from my family members. It took me many years to arrive at that place of acceptance, because sometimes God allows things to happen that make no sense at the time. But as the years pass, we learn to be grateful, even for the cave. By going through this experience, I learned that God was my ultimate protector and that I had an invisible fortress shielding me. That was the invisible hand of God. He protects, keeps, and watches over us, even when it appears we are desperate and alone.

My sister and I were united under one roof, even though it was the roof of a stranger. And in time, I would be reunited with my mother, but I would be returned to her a far different child from the one who ran away. I would return to her a child with unshakable faith. This was a hard time in my life, but it made my faith more solid. After all, diamonds can be formed only under tremendous pressure, and gold needs hot fire to be made pure. The situations of our lives may be desperate, but God uses each one selectively and carefully to make us into who He intends us to be. The pain of being ripped from the arms of my family was traumatic for me as a child, but as an adult I see it was this pain that made me strong. It taught me to see invisible walls and feel intangible support. It taught me that my life was hidden in God, and no man, no judge, no social worker, and no parent could pluck me out of the palm of His hand. This was a light developed only in the shadows. This was my cave of Adullam. Even though I didn't know it at the time, I never would have learned that type of faith, that level of God-consciousness, had I been raised by my father's family. I learned from the things I suffered, and today I am thankful for every one.

HARD PLACES MAKE FOR HARDY PEOPLE

Since moving to Colorado, I have learned to hike. I started about a year ago, so I am far from an expert, and I am not yet ready to display my skills, as I am quite embarrassed by how out of shape I am on the trails. But I love being outdoors, especially because the sedentary life of a pastor requires some new ways to exercise to help keep my weight down and my body active. I like to head out early on my days off and find a well-worn trail. Armed only with a water bottle and really comfortable shoes, I will select an easy trail that is far from dangerous. But I also want one that is challenging enough that I have to concentrate and cannot think of anything else. It is an escape from the pressures of my global ministry.

I like the feeling of having a canopy of trees over my head and hearing the babbling of clear, cold Colorado streams as I walk along. I like challenging my body to find the next place to put my foot and the next place to grasp with my hand. I adapt to the terrain as I pray inwardly, cultivating my own practical spirituality as I walk with Him in silence and solitude.

When I first started hiking, I found it very difficult. Denver is known as the Mile High City, so you know what the altitude is. For me, finding enough oxygen to climb the higher trails was so strenuous that I felt that my lungs would explode. My leg muscles would burn and the sun seemed so close to my forehead that I would be sweaty just moments after I started the hike. Often I would have to slow my pace, and sometimes I would have to come to a full stop while I desperately tried to catch my breath. Many times I would turn around on the trail, not wanting to get overextended. But as my body acclimated to the altitude, my hikes began to get longer and easier. I'm still a long way from an Ironman competition, and I haven't invited anyone to watch my struggle to breathe, but I can see my own progress. I have seen my strength and endurance increase, my lung capacity expand, and my heart become more ready for the task. I have not finished many trails, but I am getting closer to my goal. Each time I hike, I feel better and stronger. The hard way is making me hardier.

The cave of Adullam was a hard place, but it only made David better. He went in there a fugitive from Saul but left there a captain of some four hundred men. The cave transformed not only David but his men as well. They went from being broken to being mighty, and the hardness of their situation was what made them mighty.

The cave is a hard place, but it is a place of personal transformation. Only God can take the worst moments of our lives and from those fragments manufacture faith. Only God can turn pain into power and chaos into confidence. He reveals Himself to us in the caves of our lives. But He also reveals us to ourselves in these hard places. We can gauge our strength to climb up the hard way only by climbing up the hard way. And in this way, we discover how resilient and strong we really are. It is hard to be thankful while gasping for breath and hanging on to a tree, trying not to fall down. But after we have stretched ourselves far beyond what we imagined our breaking point to be, we can be thankful for how strong we have become. We cannot get stronger without struggle. The struggle is what gives us more strength. We shouldn't curse the struggle no matter how hard, because it equips us to climb higher.

ANOTHER CAVE

The cave of Adullam reminds me of another cave in the Scriptures. This cave is also found in the territory of Judah but is located about twenty miles east of the cave of Adullam. This cave is also not a natural cave. Picks, axes, and strong backs were used to remove the stone to make a suitable dwelling place for its inhabitants. This cave, carved out long after the ancient fortress that housed David, was cleaved from the rock to be the final resting place for a rich man's body.

The man's name was Joseph of Arimathea, and he had a tomb created for him in approximately AD 36. However, he would not get to use his tomb first. This cave would be "loaned" to Christ Jesus, called the son of David. Jesus just borrowed the cave, as He needed it for only three days before He emerged from that place, never to return.

It strikes me that although these two caves are removed from each other by distance and time, they served the same purpose in the lives of their inhabitants. David went into his cave a fugitive and a criminal, and so did Jesus when Rome judged Him to be insubordinate to the rulers of His day. Just as Saul thought David had designs upon his crown, the high priest thought Jesus was a threat to his power. David and the Son of David both went into their respective caves as criminals, but both came out as captains. David became the captain of his mighty men; Jesus became the captain of the host of heaven.

Both caves attracted the people who loved their inhabitants. The family of David met him at his cave, and the women who loved Jesus came as soon as the law of the Sabbath allowed them to be there. The women came to minister to Jesus when He seemed to be powerless. Similarly, David's family came to him when it seemed he was at his weakest state. Peter and John came out of hiding to look into the mouth of the empty tomb for themselves. They were broken men who left everything to follow Jesus and feared for their lives once He was sealed in the cave. These broken disciples remind me of the men who came to the cave of Adullam also defeated but left that cave mighty. Peter and John and all the disciples who came to the empty cave of Christ would become the mighty men and women God would empower to turn the world upside down.

In both caves, the broken would become mighty and the root of Jesse would bring contentment to the bitter soul (Rom. 15:12). You, too, can find peace and joy by believing in the power of an empty cave.

8

KEILAH

The City of Betrayal

David was hiding with about six hundred of his mighty men in the forest of Hareth (his numbers had grown by another two hundred mighty men after being obedient to God and leaving the cave of Adullam) when he received word that the Philistines had attacked the city of Keilah, an ancient city in the lowlands of Judah. Keilah was situated northwest of the city of Hebron, led by Joshua. Scholars disagree about the city's exact location, but the Bible is clear that this city was fortified, having strong gates and walls. The name Keilah in Hebrew means "citadel," so it is safe to assume that it was a fortress of some sort. But these structural reinforcements did little to help the city's people defend it from the Philistine invaders.

David had left the cave of Adullam after receiving prophetic instruction. The prophet Gad made the trek to the cave to tell David that it was no longer God's will for him to stay there. The prophet told him it was time for him and the entire company to leave the cave and head back into the region of Judah (1 Sam. 22:5). Gad's words might not have been welcomed initially because

David and his family members had progressed and developed well within the fortress, but David was always open to hearing the voice of prophets.

Saul was a crafty general and could use the fortress against David. Saul's army pulled from all of Israel, so he would have had massive troops at his disposal. He could have surrounded the cave and cut David off from both resources and support. Fortresses are not necessarily the safest places to be when facing an army of overwhelming numbers, as one could become a sitting duck trapped in the place designed to protect. Saul was a strong enough tactician to exploit that type of situation. He had not yet been informed that David was in the cave, but if he had been, he would have sent the army of Israel to besiege David. (We later learn that he used this very tactic when he discovered that David had come into the fortress of Keilah.)

So God sent Gad to David to alert him that he must leave Adullam because it was far safer to be mobile than to be rooted in a fortified place where he would be cut off and starved out. David and his people packed up their supplies and headed back into the open territory of Judah.

David wanted to help the people of Keilah, but he had an untested army of about six hundred men. The cave could not contain the number of people God intended David to lead, so He needed David to move out if He was going to maximize his potential.

When we are obedient in leaving our caves, we increase our capacity to grow. Whenever God gives us instruction, it is always so we can be increased either spiritually or numerically. His plan for us is always for our good, even if His instructions scare us. Don't allow fear to keep you in a safe place. If God moves you out, it is because He knows that you have a greater capacity that will be limited if you stay where you are.

David cared for his parents by sending them off to Moab, using his family's connection to the Moabites to ensure safety. David did not stay in Moab, although he easily could have claimed the same family connection. It is interesting that he did not want his aged parents to live with him on the run from Saul. This care for his mother reminds us of Jesus, who, even on the threshold of death, secured a safe haven for His own mother in the household of the apostle John. Even in the darkness of His crucifixion, Jesus's love for His mother shone through, and we see this same love in the care David gave his father and mother. David left his parents in Moab and then led Saul away from them by heading back into dangerous territory.

Unfortunately, we are sometimes safer in the company of unbelievers than we are in the company of people who pray to the same God. Sometimes we are given more help from the heathen than from the people who claim our same faith. When politics and the quest for status come into play, they can ruin alliances and cause people to break covenantal connections. This was the case with Saul. David's parents were safer in the territory of the Moabite king than they were in the territory of the king of Israel.

I have seen this dynamic in the church. Some people have been so hurt by Christian leaders that they feel safer in the company of those who have no faith at all. I have had to learn how to minister to this tragedy over the years because so many people join our churches but are still hurting from what happened in their past church experiences. Often I have to lay down what another Christian leader has done to damage the confidence these people once had in their leaders. And, sadly, David could not trust his leader to treat his parents fairly, so it was better to trust the heathen.

From Moab, David sojourned into the forest of Hareth and hid with his band of mighty men. The exact location is lost to us, except we know it was in the territory of Judah. They no longer had the cave of Adullam to give them the illusion of safety, yet they were fully mobile and able to escape King Saul's army. While David was in the forest, he heard that the Philistines had attacked Keilah. This is when David entered his next city and learned the next vital lesson any person who seeks to reach their fullest potential must learn: how to survive betrayal. David's test of betrayal was given in the classroom of Keilah.

A CALL FOR HELP

Not only did the Philistines break through the defenses of Keilah, but they timed their attack to coincide with the harvest. They waited to attack until the farmers were in the process of threshing their wheat and breached the citadel to steal the harvest from the threshing floors of the city. The Philistines did not attack when the harvest was still in the fields; they had no desire to work to bring the harvest in.

The Enemy is strategic in this way; he always seeks to attack us when we are at the point of harvest. The battles will intensify in your life at the moments when you are just about to reap what you have been patiently cultivating. The fact that the battle has escalated should not discourage you; it is an indication that you are closer to the blessing God has planned for you than ever before.

The Philistines were able to penetrate the citadel and take advantage of Keilah because Saul was preoccupied with hunting David. He did not prioritize the safety of this city over his pursuit of David. The king was so caught up in defending his title and his position that he did not fulfill the duties that go along with that title. Leaders are on the wrong path when they are more concerned with fighting false threats to their authority than with preserving the lives and livelihoods of the people they are charged to defend. Leaders of organizations, churches, businesses, and even families can become so preoccupied by dealing with internal matters that the real Enemy is allowed to sneak in uncontested and steal the harvest.

The men of Keilah were unable to defend their city even though their gates and walls were still intact. The Philistines had overrun the city. The wives and children of Keilah were left undefended, and King Saul seemingly had no concern for them. This dereliction of duty was another indicator that he was no longer fit to lead. Saul was so far gone that he did not answer the cry of the people of Keilah and rush to their defense. David, however, could not ignore the cries for help that came from Keilah, even though it was not yet his responsibility to be their defender. He showed that he had the heart of a true servant-leader even before he was crowned as the leader of these people. Leadership is not for people who don't love people, as authority reveals true motives and exposes character.

Last September there was a fire in an apartment complex in the neighborhood around our church in Denver. When the fire broke out in the dead of night, people were awakened by the smell of smoke. They leaped from their beds, grabbed their children, and ran for their lives. In some areas, the fire was so hot and dangerous that people jumped from their second-story windows to escape. Families poured out of fire escapes with just the clothes on their backs while the firefighters fought valiantly to extinguish the fire. Some fifty families had to find shelter outside of their homes while the engineers inspected the building to see if it was safe for them to return. In the meantime, the families needed a warm place to stay.

Our church has cultivated a good working relationship with our local fire chief, so at four in the morning, he called our facilities manager to see if the families could be sheltered in our church's banquet hall. Our facilities manager answered his call and had our twenty-four-hour on-site security team open the buildings and prepare to receive them. I was not aware of the need until about an hour later when I woke up for my morning prayer and checked in with my office. By that time, the Red Cross had already come to set up emergency cots beneath the crystal chandeliers in our church banquet hall. Our church food bank ministry was already packing bags filled with emergency groceries and toiletries, and our café workers were brewing hot coffee to help keep everyone warm. No one called me to ask if it was okay. They have all worked with me long enough to know that one of my deepest prayers for our church is that we will always be sensitive to the needs of people and respond to them. You cannot truly lead a community if you are deaf to people's pleas. You cannot truly lead a community you are unwilling to serve. Our resources are limited, but our prayer is that we will always do our best to serve the people.

The victims and even the Red Cross workers wouldn't stop thanking me for opening the doors of our church. But as I hugged the little kids, shook hands, and made sure everyone had received a bag of groceries, I couldn't stop myself from thanking *them*. Their need is what gives us purpose, and their cry is the truest indication of the condition of our hearts. I was proud that on that cold, dark morning, we all passed the test.

David passed this test as well. He heard the cries of the men of Keilah and wanted to come to their defense. He wanted to come to their aid even though he was just a fugitive running from an evil king. His present position did not dictate his desire to act. And Christ Jesus proved His right to be our leader, not because He defended His position and title but because He was willing to lay down His life for us. His sacrifice on the cross demonstrated His incredible love for us and His true heart of a leader. Great leaders are servants of the people, not just title seekers interested only in defending their positions.

PRAY BEFORE BATTLE

David wanted to come to the aid of the people of Keilah, but he prayed first before going to battle. This is important for us to note, because too often we engage in battles we have not first prayed about. David was brave, valiant, skilled, and anointed, but he also had the wisdom to seek the Lord. We did not see him do this when he faced Goliath in the valley of Elah. He did not consult with a

priest or seek out the advice of a prophet before challenging the
Philistines; he rushed headlong into the fray. But in the valley of
Elah, he was faced with one-on-one combat. In this case, he was a
captain responsible for the lives of his men. His men were untested
in battle and quite fearful. This time he sought the Lord before he
made his move.

The more people we are responsible for leading, the greater our
prayer lives must be. When leading a church, an organization, or a
family, we must pray before moving, because other lives are at stake.
We may have the faith to face our enemies, tackle the problem, or
confront the challenge, but wisdom dictates that we temper our
courage with prayer. Seeking the Lord for the right timing to do
something is not cowardice; it is wise. Maturity teaches us that we
have to make prayer-filled decisions when others can be adversely
affected by the decisions we make. Doing things at the right time
is often the difference between triumph and disaster, and prayer is
the only way to know for sure that we are in God's timing.

David teaches us that we are foolish to move forward without accessing the power of prayer. After seeking the Lord, David
decided to come to the rescue of the people of Keilah. His rag-
tag band of broken men was being shaped into a small army
as David led them into battle. He was experienced in fighting
the Philistines, but his troops were not, so they were afraid to
face the experienced army of invaders. They were already afraid
of Saul and his army, but David would not allow them to be
concerned with just their own defense; he led them to use their
strength to help others. The mighty men were so frightened that
David sought the Lord a second time, and only after he received

the second confirmation did they have the confidence to face the Philistines.

David's troops succeeded, so much so that they were able to take the Philistines' cattle away and for the first time receive the spoils of battle. After prayer, the mighty men of David began to live up to that title by facing their own fears and were encouraged by the results. David pushed his small army to discover who they really were, and God gave them an amazing first victory.

Without the confidence that comes from prayer, we can be intimidated by enemies we actually are able to defeat. We cannot become mighty without facing struggle. Through struggle we advance, and through facing opposition we begin to discover how strong we really are. The mighty are often unaware of their own strength until they are put in positions where they are challenged and then overcome. The victors receive the spoils, but only if they attempt to win. Our self-esteem and self-identity must be grounded in God, but they are buttressed by the things we overcome.

David and his men marched back through the gates of Keilah as the victors. David was the savior and received the appreciation of the people. Imagine the parade of people who greeted him at the city gates: the singing and dancing of the women as they celebrated the harvest that was safe in their barns. But the parade was short-lived. News that David was in the city spread so far that Saul heard of the success and believed this was his opportunity to trap David. David's service to the people of Keilah became the occasion where his enemy tried to destroy him.

Often our successes alert our enemies to our location. It is interesting to see how many times Jesus told the people He helped not to tell anyone it was He who helped them. The word of the miraculous works of Jesus was told to the people who celebrated His success as well as to the people who were opposed to His ministry. Some people came to Jesus to be healed, but His enemies came to criticize His ministry and set traps for Him. The Pharisees were in that crowd. They came to stifle His ministry, not to celebrate it. When we are doing good work, we often are surprised by the attacks that our good work attracts. But we must not be discouraged from helping, because only through helping others do we discover how mighty we can become.

GATES AND WALLS

Saul was not intimidated by the walls of the citadel housing David; he saw the fortress as a way to ensnare David. King Saul intended to surround David and cut off the city from being resupplied. This was a standard tactic that the generals of David's time would have used when facing an army entrenched behind city walls. The idea was to starve out the inhabitants until they were forced to surrender. If they could hold them in their own stronghold long enough, it would cause them to turn on themselves and eventually someone would open the gates. Saul sprang into action. He had no intention of fighting David in an open field; he believed his tactic could bring about a bloodless victory for him.

This is a situation that can occur when we are dependent on gates and walls. The very things we intend to protect us can turn into the things that keep us from being free. We build walls around our hearts to protect us from being hurt, but these emotional walls can also keep us from receiving love. We can be so guarded that we don't allow others to penetrate our protective layers. In our pain, it is hard to realize that the heart is stronger than we ever could imagine; it can recover from horrible disappointments and learn to love again.

The Enemy can exploit those walls and cut us off from the freedom God intends for us to experience. We can become so involved in an ideology, a theology, a role, or even a career that we forfeit the freedom to move on to something better. Sometimes the gates that were intended to protect us become the bars that hold us in. Then we have to take the bold risk of leaving what once was a safe place and venture into what is unknown. Freedom is not free. It always requires the high cost of risk. We have to leave the walls of safety to maintain the freedom of mobility that God intends for us.

Our lives, even as believers, cannot be limited to the four walls of our churches, or those walls will hinder us from having an impact in our world. Jesus went to the synagogue every Sabbath, but the rest of the week He was found in the city squares and streets. He was always surrounded by sinners and tax collectors, and He dined with people the religious leaders of His day would not dare to break bread with.

I believe that Christians should go to church, but we should also serve and lead in our communities so the love of Jesus can be seen in our world. We cannot let religious walls keep us from venturing out and influencing our world. Those walls are too small to house the amazing love of Jesus, and they are too small to house the personal impact one person can have on the world.

At our church in Denver, we have always supported and operated a food pantry as one of the ministries. When I moved to Denver, I made sure we partnered with our local food bank, even though it was a secular organization. We decided early on that we would not limit our services to our own church members. We recognized that hunger has no color, no faith, and no ethnicity. It's is a human condition the church was commanded by Jesus to heal, regardless of the circumstances. By tearing down those religious walls, we quickly saw our community regard the church not as an inaccessible fortress but as a resource and legitimate partner. We wanted them to see that we were open to serve the city. We refused to be walled in.

Pray Again

Confronted with the news that Saul had heard he was in Keilah, David returned to prayer. As providence would have it, the priest Abiathar had also heard David was in the city and rallied to his side. Saul had killed Abiathar's father, Ahimelech (1 Sam. 22:16–21), whose only crime was innocently assisting David in his escape by giving him bread from the tabernacle and the sword of Goliath. Because of this, Abiathar decided to align himself with David. But this priest did not come empty-handed; he came with an ephod (23:6). A sign of kingly authority, an ephod was a special uniform with jewels in it. These jewels, called urim and thummim, were considered a godly way to seek guidance for a yes or no answer. As we'll later learn, this contrasts greatly with Saul's use of a witch to foretell the outcome of what would be his last battle. With this ephod, David was able, by means that aren't clear, to better discern the will of God. Throughout David's journey, as he was eluding King Saul, he consulted this ephod. Although we don't quite know how God communicated with him through the ephod, we do see time after time that the ephod was never wrong. Saul's murderous attack against someone who inadvertently assisted David created an avenue for David to repeatedly receive greater assistance from the Lord. What Saul meant for evil, God turned into good for David.

What I love is that David took time to pray again before moving. As we develop into the people God desires us to become, we need to stay open to hearing new instruction from Him. Too often, we follow old commands instead of listening for new directions. The children of Israel, while on their forty-year sojourn through the wilderness, had to follow the cloud and the pillar. They were given no road map to the Promised Land. They just had to daily watch for where God was leading them.

God had told David to go to Keilah and fight the Philistines. It was a great word of direction, and they were successful. But now the situation had changed and David needed to pray again. Every change requires a check-in for new instructions. Had David assumed that God wanted him to stay in Keilah, he would have risked disaster. Had he relied on the loyalty of the inhabitants of Keilah to stand up against Saul, he would have been gravely disappointed. Their well of gratitude ran so shallow that God told David that the men of Keilah would "deliver him up."

David is noted as a great military warrior, but he demonstrated that he was a prayer warrior as well. He prayed before he went in, and he prayed about whether he should stay. A loving God who is ever watchful gave him direction at every turn. He was not so confident in his own abilities or the reliability of people; his confidence was in the Lord. Prayer was the only thing that kept him from destruction, and so often the only thing that will keep us out of trouble is purposefully taking the time to pray.

LED INTO BETRAYAL

As we consider David's experience in this city, challenging questions emerge: Why would God lead David into a place to be betrayed? Why would He allow him to rescue a city of betrayers? The people of Keilah were not thankful or loyal to David. Even after he risked his life for them, they would not risk anything for him. It is easy to blame the men of Keilah for their cowardice and lack of faithfulness, but the deeper question is why God even led David into this situation at all. Certainly, God knew beforehand that the inhabitants of Keilah were not worthy of David's help, but He still guided David to risk his life and rush to their defense.

Asking God why is no sin; it is a perfectly human response. We must not be afraid to question what we do not understand in our lives. God is not intimidated by our questions. And if having questions was a sin, then Job could never have been called righteous. It is possible to be obedient and still question. It is possible to have surrendered and still wonder exactly what God is doing. It is not that faith never asks questions; it is that faith never stops being obedient while asking questions.

Even David asked in the Psalms, "My God, my God, why hast thou forsaken me?" (22:1). These words were echoed by our Christ as He died in agony on the cross (Matt. 27:46). If it was acceptable for David to question, it is all right for us also. If it was okay for Jesus to question His Father and speak out of the depths of His own humanity, then it must be all right for us to ask God important things, even as we walk by faith.

The "why" questions have great significance to me because I've asked plenty of them about my own life. Why would God allow me to be removed from the safe home of my aunt and uncle and be placed in foster care? Why would He allow me to go through that world-shaking experience and feel as if the universe and God ultimately had forsaken me? Why would God teach me lessons through such a confidence-breaking experience at such a young age when He could have taught me another way?

In my own way—in the language of a frightened eight-year-old boy—I wiped away invisible tears I was too angry and too hurt to allow to run down my brown cheeks. I simply asked the Lord, *Why? I still believe in You, but why, Lord? I am still walking by faith, but why do I have to walk through this? Why can't I just be like the normal kids I saw in the library and the ones I saw at the elementary school who live with their own families? Why do I have to fight off rats at night and do favors for drug dealers for spare money? Why can't I be one of the kids who eat three meals a day and sleep in real beds and have never left and lost all sense of home?*

"Why, Lord?" It is a great question—one that the eight-year-old me had no answer for but one I could answer for him now. If I could get a message back to myself—if I had a time machine and could whisper into my own ear to tell Little Chris the future—I would say, "This is all for your own good." If I could put a message in a bottle and float it safely across the seas of time, I would tell myself, "This situation is only going to make you better." I would say, "You will be sensitive to the needs of the hungry because you have known hunger. You will hear the cries of the orphan because you have been orphaned. You will fearlessly father your own bio-logical sons because you know what it is to have no father. You will spiritually foster sons and daughters in the ministry because you have been fostered." I would tell myself, "Each step of your life—the back steps, the bad steps, and the missteps—will work only for your good. You will preach to people all over the world through your own tears, and they will feel the authenticity of your message not because they know your story but because they feel that you are a survivor of your own battle."

God led David into betrayal for one reason: the spoils. Scripture tells us that not only did David and his mighty men defeat the Philistines but they also recovered the Philistines' cattle. Those cattle did not belong to the men of Keilah; they belonged to the Philistines. So they became the property of David and his mighty men immediately after the battle. The cattle and the victory over the enemy, not the loyalty of Keilah, were the reward for obeying God and going to this city (1 Sam. 23:5). Sometimes we misunderstand what the spoils of a city really are. Only by prayerful contemplation and careful reexamination of our lives are we able to discern them. What did we win from every city? What did we gain from every loss? Why was the pain important, and what did God intend for us to learn about ourselves and about Him? Each city leaves us with a new experience and a greater understanding.

THESE ARE THE SPOILS

God led David to Keilah to unleash his troops on the Philistines and allow the mighty men to discover that they were no longer broken men who needed to live in fear of the vast army of Saul. They truly were becoming mighty and were confirmed in their understanding that they had an anointed captain in David and that God was indeed directing his path. God also led David to Keilah so he could capture the Philistines' livestock to enrich his camp.

Remember, many of the mighty men came to David heavily in debt. In Keilah, they began to see that their financial situation was going to change under the leadership of David. Their captain was going to leave them better off than they were when he found them. Through their allegiance to David, they would also receive spoils. This set a significant precedent for David and his troops. When they fought for David, they walked away with tangible goods. This is important, because too often we fight battles that produce no spoils. Fighting battles that lead to no gain is exhausting. Working so hard with nothing to show for it can be discouraging. But working hard in battle and then walking away holding the leash of a living, breathing animal would have been incredibly empowering for these men.

Discerning the spoils after you have gone through a betrayal can be difficult. But if God leads you into the place of betrayal, then the spoils are always present. Sometimes it just takes time for us to realize they are there. Joseph was betrayed by his brothers and sold into Egypt. The spoils of his betrayal were gaining the second-highest position in all of Egypt and the deliverance of his family. And Jesus is our key example of this Keilah situation. He was betrayed by the people He came to save. He healed and helped people for three years. He demonstrated love and provision to every open heart, and still they betrayed Him. The same crowd He served so well willingly traded His life for the release of the notorious criminal Barabbas, leading to Jesus's crucifixion under Pontius Pilate. Even one of His own disciples was duplicitous. Interestingly, the man who sold out Jesus was named after the same tribe the men of Keilah descended from. Judas is the Greek form of Judah.

We can be certain that the spoils of His betrayal were not to receive the loyalty of those He came to save; His spoils were in defeating the Enemy and recovering the herd. The nail-scarred hand of our Master held the leash of lost humanity and led us safely away. We are no longer the property of the Enemy, because Jesus came to take captivity captive and set us free (Eph. 4:7–10). I am so glad to be in His herd.

AN INGLORIOUS EXIT

Informed by the Lord of Saul's intentions and the imminent betrayal of the men of the city, David decided to leave Keilah. There certainly were no parades as he and his troops exited. The women probably were no longer singing. Scripture says David and his men "arose and departed" (1 Sam. 23:13). The word *depart* is *yatsa* in the Hebrew, and it means "to exit." The abrupt exit of David from the city is also instructive for us. Sometimes we are not given a lot of warning when transition comes into our lives. Sometimes there is no memo dispatched, no severance package given, and no grief counselor available. No parade, no party, no appreciation—it's just over. David took his troops and their spoils, and they quit the city. They had no destination and no real plan; they just exited the city because this stage was over.

When the city of betrayal ends abruptly, please let it end. You do a greater disservice to yourself if you do not move out of that city and let that city move out of you. Betrayal is inevitable. Most of us have experienced it already, and all of us will experience it as we progress to what God has promised us. Don't allow what you went through to discourage you from going forward. David did not allow what he experienced in Keilah to stop him from helping people. He did not build walls and gates around his own heart, stop loving people, or stop trusting God. He exited Keilah ingloriously, but he did exit.

When God allows you to go through a season of betrayal, take your spoils and leave. Don't allow the pain of your Keilah to prevent you from trusting people. Don't allow your past pain to predict your future. You don't want to miss one gift, relationship, or opportunity that God has intended for you to experience or encounter. Just quietly exit your Keilah and live to love, trust, fight, learn, and lead another day.

9

EN GEDI

The City of Revenge

Imagine walking past a deep dark-blue sea of salt. The harsh sun beats down upon your face. There is no breeze to cool you, and there are no clouds to shade you. You walk on ancient brown sand, so fine it feels like baby powder under your feet. Each step kicks it all the way up to your knees.

The reddish-brown hillocks and sparse vegetation make you wonder if you are still on earth, but our familiar yellow sun beams down upon your forehead with a harsh heat, reminding you that you're still on this planet. Salty, stinging sweat runs into your squinting eyes. You are at the lowest place on earth that a human can walk without an oxygen mask. The place you find yourself is the Dead Sea.

The Dead Sea is a hypersalinated lake situated in the Jordan Rift Valley. It is tucked between modern-day Israel and Palestine to the east and the nation of Jordan to the west. We call it the Dead Sea, but the Bible called it Yam HaMelach, the Sea of Salt. Its surface and shores are about 1,400 feet below sea level, making it the lowest elevation on land. Its salinity is more than 33 percent, almost nine times saltier than the Atlantic Ocean. It is so salty that no animal can live in its waters. No schools of fish swim in it, and natural asphalt floats upon the still surface.

The Jordan River ends its flow at the Dead Sea, which has no outflow. The burning sun evaporates its waters, with each year seemingly hotter than the last. In one year, the sky yields less than four inches of rain because the Judean Mountains prevent the storm clouds from moving across this parched valley. The sea's water is so salty that no one can swim in it properly. One just floats in it, unable to stay submerged for long.

David, the outlaw, had run here trying to evade King Saul. His band of mighty men walked their newly acquired cattle past the Dead Sea's poisonous shores. The sun chased them as relentlessly as the demon-driven king. Rocky, cave-pocked hills guarded the way to their right, so they walked beside the shore with their rear guard carefully searching the horizon for Saul's scouts. The harsh sun burned their skin darker as they marched on beside this sea of death. They could walk into the water to cool themselves but could not drink it.

They continued on until they reached a specific turn on the ancient road. About two-thirds of the way between the caves that would one day hide the scrolls and the natural mountain fortress from which King Herod would carve his Masada, there was a shout. It was a shout of joy that rang out through the ranks of the mighty men as they finally reached the oasis. They started to run toward the sound of the waterfall, and bleating, thirsty sheep followed close after them. The green, spring-fed water brought life and laughter to all.

David had made it to the spring of the goats and the caves of En Gedi. The hard, dry caves and mountains would become his hiding place. He moved his troops from the woods into the mountains, struggling to find food and water to support their numbers. But Saul was relentless in his pursuit. He was hell-bent on killing David and had received word that he was hiding in the region's strongholds. The king had assembled a force of three thousand men—a force large enough to overwhelm David's numbers but small enough to keep up the chase. King Saul was dominated by one thought: to capture and kill David and secure his own throne. It is amazing that Saul could not see David as anything but a threat when he had done nothing to threaten his reign or challenge his authority. People often perceive others as threats, painting them with their own motives and allowing their delusions to obscure reality.

Saul drew so close that he actually walked into the very same cave where David was hiding, and they had a face-to-face encounter. The Bible is quite graphic in describing how Saul entered the cave to use the bathroom, leaving his guards behind so he could have privacy. The guards were positioned outside the cave while Saul's enemy hid inside. Saul had no armor and had laid aside his sword. His royal guard gave him the distance he needed to do his business in peace, not knowing that David was there (1 Sam. 24).

I have stood before these caves, and they are so numerous that the likelihood of Saul's selecting this particular cave to relieve himself is statistically off the charts. In the darkness, David's mighty men whispered to him that surely this must be the hand of God placing the king within their grasp. To them, this was a prophetic moment when David could come out of the shadows and kill the king and they could all safely return to their homes victorious. Having no loyalty to Saul, they saw this as a perfect opportunity to put this mad king to death. But David was of another spirit. He refused to kill Saul in the cave. He would not touch a hair on his head, because he still recognized Saul as the Lord's anointed. He would not kill Saul then or ever. He would rather run from this killer than kill him, and this decision was the truest test of this city: the city of revenge.

Moving Too Soon

Life has so many different streets and avenues to choose from that it can be daunting to have to prayerfully discern which path to take and make the key decisions to move toward your own purpose. One can become paralyzed trying to analyze the choices presented. Real life is not easy or neat, and there are seldom just two clear options. It is easy to become paralyzed in indecision, fearing making the wrong choice.

I have known many undergraduate college students who changed their majors each year in an attempt to select just the right career path. They'd jump from one discipline to the next, seeking the perfect decision, only prolonging the process of their education and often getting themselves deeper into debt. I have known men who vacillated between women, so afraid of picking the wrong spouse that they delayed making a commitment to anyone. These men often waited so long that Ms. Right decided to move on and stop waiting. I have watched people move from job to job, from city to city, and from church to church, so determined to find the perfect place that they missed the opportunity to experience the good in any situation. After all, God's perfect situation doesn't always look perfect at the time. Navigating the seas of our own destiny can be difficult. Sometimes what feels bad to us is good for us, but God perfects us through the imperfect situations of our lives. We can move too soon to avoid discomfort, not realizing that God is using discomfort to develop us in important ways.

Making key decisions for ourselves can be hard, but I didn't know what to do when faced with making an even harder choice for my father. I remember walking through the airport in Dallas when a doctor called me from the veterans hospital in Augusta, Georgia—the city of my ancestors for four generations. I recognized the area code, so I picked up the call right away. This was the same area code of my paternal grandmother, who used to call me each month. Although she had passed from this life (a victim of breast cancer) a few years before, I was conditioned to respond to a number with this area code.

The doctor stated his name and said he was calling because my father, Ernest Hill, had listed my name as his only next of kin. He had left written instructions that I was to make any critical decisions regarding his medical care in the event that he was unable to make decisions for himself. He had not told me he had entrusted me with this responsibility, so I was shocked into silence even as the clipped tones of a military doctor explained my father's condition and asked for my orders.

My father had been rushed to the hospital because the steroids he had been prescribed by his doctors for years to treat one condition had caused him to develop type 2 diabetes. Somehow his insulin levels had gotten out of control, and one of his cousins had found him passed out on the floor of his home. She had called an ambulance to take him to the hospital. The doctors and nurses had done all they could to stabilize him, but my father had slipped into a diabetic coma. The doctor informed me that my father had been in that condition long enough that they needed to get directives from me as his next of kin. Should they pull the plug and let him die, or did I want them to leave him on the machines that were keeping him alive?

I suddenly was faced with the decision of whether he lived or died—the man who had left me before I was born, the man had who had never given me a penny to take care of my needs. He had never shown any interest in my health, education, or career. This was the man who did not assert his parental privilege to pull his two children out of the foster home but instead left us in a system and watched passively as I was bandied about in the courts. As far as I knew, this man never cared if I even lived or died. Now the doctor was asking me to decide if I wanted my father to live or die.

I was not even forty years old and had to make a life-or-death decision about my deadbeat father. Our family had not had careful and prayerful deliberation about these issues. My father had just written my name on a sheet of paper, bypassing his own cousins who knew him better and instead thrusting the fate of his life into my hands.

LOVING THE UNLOVABLE

This was a great test for me, because I had already done so much heart work and soul searching to forgive this man for all he had inflicted. He had left so much pressure on my mother that she crumbled under the weight of raising us without any paternal support. When he went away, my sister, Marie, knew who he was and what it was to have a father in her life. To me, this was an even worse fate than my own, because I didn't have a father to miss. I resented him for rejecting me, but my real anger was over what he had done to my sister. Marie had the memories of his presence implanted in her heart and felt the loss like a rusted knife stabbing her soul daily.

Over the years, I had struggled within myself to forgive him. I'd dug deep into the well of God's grace just to talk to him each time his mother had handed him the phone, especially because I knew she was forcing him to talk to me. I had to decide continually to forgive the man each time I was faced with a decision that required the counsel of a father, knowing I had no real father to turn to.

I had to forgive him for not being present at any of the key moments of my life, such as when I taught myself how to tie a tie and to drive a car. I had to forgive him when I filled out college admission forms by myself, knowing that he was a college graduate and was even enrolled in graduate school. This man was being trained to educate people and couldn't be bothered to help me get my education. I had to forgive him each time I struggled to buy a college textbook. I had to forgive him each time I rode my bicycle to the fast-food restaurants where I worked to pay my way through college. I rode my bike down the snowy streets of Boston while he was driving in a warm car in the sultry southern heat of Augusta. I forgave him on every birthday when he didn't send a card. I had to forgive him for not being there to help me select my tux for the senior prom or for my wedding day and not helping me pay for either occasion. I had to forgive him for not showing me how to be a man and a father. When the doctors handed me my firstborn son, I felt profoundly ill-equipped to raise a son because I had never had a father to raise me. I had to find my own way and trust the Lord to give me the wisdom to know what to do.

Forgiveness is never a onetime event; it is an ongoing process. It is never a single moment in time; it is a progressive work of human grace. My study of the Scriptures has taught me that we must struggle to extend grace to people, even the people who don't deserve that grace. That's because God has extended His greater grace to us by the work of the cross—a grace we do not and could never deserve.

Harboring unforgiveness is dangerous, because God promises to remit our sins only if we forgive those who trespass against us (Matt. 6:14–15). I knew my sins were so numerous that I desperately needed God to extend His forgiveness to me, but this is hard work—daily, gut-wrenching work. The Holy Spirit will enable us to do it, but He can assist us only if we are willing. In those hurtful moments when we realize we have every reason to fan the flame of unforgiveness, we must douse the fire with the water of grace before it burns a hole in our hearts.

Christianity is not a religion; it is a faith that requires us to believe in the sovereignty of God. Religion is man's attempt to reach God through a system of acts, but Christianity is faith that a loving God has come to reach us. Christianity requires faith in the love of God in order to experience all of its benefits. Jesus teaches us to turn the other cheek, love our enemies, and forgive those who hurt us (Matt. 5:39, 44; 6:14). To do so requires faith even when our human desire for justice might drive us to strike out and take justifiable revenge. Christianity calls us to a higher standard of forgiveness.

Jesus stood before Pontius Pilate and allowed the Roman governor to sentence Him to a bloody death on the cross. Jesus allowed the Roman soldiers to strike Him and beat Him with the cat-o'-nine-tails. At any moment, Jesus could have summoned a legion of angels to swoop down and come to His defense. He could have commanded the earth to open up and swallow His accusers or caused the governor to breathe his last breath as he spoke out his judgment. But He decided to demonstrate forgiveness that brought healing to the world. He spent His precious last breaths beseeching the Father to forgive His assassins. His is the example of a life of grace. He was perfectly innocent of all wrong, yet He endured the punishment of guilty men to secure our salvation. Jesus was showing all mankind and even the angelic host what love looks like. The phrase "God is love" takes on real meaning when He loves the unlovable and excuses the sins of people who have not even asked to be forgiven. His love for us spoke louder than the voice of justice, and He chose to forgive. Jesus is a divine being, but here He was not operating out of the power of His divinity.

He laid down His own divine power and stood as only a man to demonstrate the power of our own free will. We, too, can choose to forgive.

To forgive like this, you must love your enemies—love them enough not to do unto them as they have done unto you. Love must follow the Golden Rule to do unto others what you would have done to you. This is the greatest example of passing the test of revenge. Jesus allowed His love of mankind to guide His decisions, showing a kind of mercy that still causes me to be awestruck.

In David, we see this same example, but David was not the Messiah, so we cannot assign to him the same divine piety. We should recognize that this was the work of a man who had dug deep inside himself and decided to forgive. David, much to the consternation and confusion of his own soldiers, decided to love the unlovable, honor the dishonorable, and allow King Saul to go free.

SET THEM FREE

When you decide to hold someone in unforgiveness, it is like building a spiritual prison in your heart. You sit upon the judgment seat of your own emotions and sentence the person to incarceration in that jail. The chains and bars, though imaginary, are stronger than Alcatraz. There is no plea bargain, no early release, and no parole. Also trapped in that prison are the memories of what that person did to you. The sound of harsh and hurting words said to you echo continually, and over and over you feel the pain of being wronged.

You become the court stenographer and list in detail each of the crimes. You decide that the person deserves to be locked up in a prison of unforgiveness for life. The big problem with this prison is that you must guard it continuously. There is a spiritual chain that attaches you to it, and you are shackled at the point of your broken heart. Not only can your heart never truly be free but it also never can heal—not as long as it is shackled to the person and the memory of what was done to you. Unforgiveness is a prison cell built for two. You become a cellmate with the person who hurt you, and your life is lived behind those spiritual bars.

I had to decide to set myself and others free, and I have spent my entire ministry career pleading with others to do the same. The criminal may not deserve forgiveness, but you deserve the freedom. The mystery of forgiveness is that when you set the other person free, you free yourself. We are connected to those we love and to those we decide to hate. Just as love is not bound by time, distance, or death, so also is unforgiveness unconquerable by these constraints. I have consoled many people who are still holding a grudge against people they no longer see. They may have moved thousands of miles away but are still in the grip of unforgiveness. They can move on physically but still be bound spiritually simply because they refuse to forgive. They have carried the hurt with them like old luggage. They carry it from house to house, state to state, and nation to nation. It is as if the soul connection also has a passport, a plane ticket, or a car to chase you into your future, poisoning it with the pain of your past. I have even sat with people who were still living with unforgiveness in their hearts toward people who had been dead for many years. I counseled them to go to grave sites with fresh flowers and release those old wounds—to unburden their souls and not allow the crimes done to them to impede a full, abundant life.

Unforgiveness creates a bond, and it also creates a wall that separates us from the grace of God. This wall prevents our powerful God from forgiving someone who has not forgiven others. The law of reaping and sowing dictates this truth (Gal. 6:7). Our God cannot break His word. If we sow seeds of unforgiveness toward others, we must reap unforgiveness in our own lives. No matter how great the crime against me, holding on to the desire for revenge is not worth allowing my own sins to be counted against me. No person, no wound merits this level of personal loss. No crime is worth holding someone in that spiritual prison if I must stay behind those bars with him.

Even though David was not yet thirty years of age, he had the wisdom to walk in this truth. He passed the real test of En Gedi: he rejected the desire to live in unforgiveness, rage, and revenge and allowed King Saul to go free. He refused to live in that toxic state. He would not kill the king; he would not take vengeance. He would not allow any of his men to sneak out of the shadows to strike down an unwitting and defenseless Saul. Saul was the Lord's anointed and David determined that as long as Saul drew breath, he would not endanger his life.

This is a spiritual lesson we must both mark and obey. "Touch not mine anointed" (Ps. 105:15) is a command that must be understood by every person hurt by church experiences. It must be embraced by people who have been disappointed by spiritual leadership and are now wrestling with the decision of how to forgive. Fallen leadership still has to be addressed with the utmost respect. David would not raise his weapon against Saul, because he understood that Saul was anointed and must not be touched lest he break Scripture and set a precedent before his own men. We cannot sow disrespect without reaping it in our own lives. Even justifiable revenge is dangerous, because acting on vengeful feelings compounds the injury and gives the criminals way too much influence over our future.

MOVING MANTLES

David did sever a corner of Saul's mantle, and either he was so stealthy or Saul was so preoccupied that the king did not detect David's drawing near. He was fulfilling a prophecy by cutting off a small portion of Saul's garments. This was the divine fulfillment of what had already transpired between King Saul and the prophet Samuel. Long before David was even anointed in Bethlehem, Saul mistakenly ripped the mantle of Samuel, triggering Samuel to prophesy that another would sit upon the throne of Israel. Even as Saul ripped the mantle off of Samuel, God ripped the kingdom out of Saul's hands. David was not present for that encounter between Saul and Samuel, but in the cave of En Gedi, he fulfilled that prophecy by cutting away a piece of Saul's mantle. He would be able to take the mantle of a king without having to shed the king's blood.

This was the Lord's judgment against Saul, and there was nothing that could be done to change or modify it (even though Samuel sought to change it). Samuel prayed for Saul with such frequency and fervency that God had to tell him to stop praying.

God told the prophet He had selected someone who would be a better king than Saul. God has the ability to move on, and we need to adopt that life skill as well. Forgiving people does not mean they still get to have the same amount of access to our lives as before; it just means we are not harboring the toxicity of unforgiveness. Mantles move and people are allowed to walk into spaces that others have been forced to vacate because of their actions. God designs things this way so we will never get stuck in relational holding patterns of being loyal to people disloyal to us.

David was convicted about even touching Saul's mantle, yet his men expected him to take off the king's head. But David understood this spiritual process, so he repented that he even touched the mantle. He need not cut away from Saul what God had already removed. God moves and removes mantles; it is His business and we don't have to be concerned with it. How many people have quit going to church entirely because they were disappointed at a particular one? The outcry against organized religion is so fierce because we have not embraced the reality that it is God who deals with unrepentant leaders. This understanding frees us from having to exact vengeance or live in unforgiveness.

THE GOD OF VENGEANCE

"Vengeance is mine; I will repay, saith the Lord" (Rom. 12:19). Most people see the God of the Bible, particularly the New Testament, as a big ol' softy. I know what it is to argue with God about why He was being so lenient with people who hurt me. I shook my fist at heaven and said, "I don't need You to be the lamb here, Jesus; I need You to be the lion." I have argued with God in prayer and asked Him to pour out some of that Old Testament wrath on my enemies. I have asked for locusts, lice, and fiery ice to be released on spiteful people. But while I am praying, He reminds me from the Scriptures that He and He alone is the arbiter of when vengeance should be released. Our God is a God of vengeance, and He refuses to share that with us. We cannot expect Him to give us New Testament grace while giving Old Testament judgment to others. We can ask, but His divine character cannot violate the principles of His Word. He expects us to pray for our enemies. He expects us to rejoice when people misuse us, because we are most like Jesus when we are forgiving the sins of people who do not deserve it. Be assured that in due season, He will deal with every unrepentant person who has done you evil. His justice is relentless, but His patience is eternal.

It is easy to trust Him to oversee mercy, but we have a much harder time entrusting vengeance to Him. We must, like David, choose to forgive and eject all bitterness from our hearts, allowing God to do what He alone is qualified to do.

Another Ending

My father had been sick for more than twenty years, most of that time physically disabled and in a wheelchair. With my grand-mother and grandfather both deceased, he had been forced to care for himself for the last year. He was a large man, so home health aides had difficulty looking after him. His affairs were almost all in order, and perhaps the best thing was for the doctors to keep him comfortable. I must admit that deep in the darkest corners of my broken heart, I wanted to tell them just to pull the plug on my father and by my own word eradicate from this world one of the most selfish, cruel people who had ever lived. In that dark and broken place in my heart, I wanted vengeance. In that instance, I wanted to even the score. And then it was gone. I realized I had fought too hard to forgive this man and free myself from the toxicity of unforgiveness. I knew that God had given me so much grace that even the things I never received from my biological father I had received from my heavenly Father in ways that far exceeded my wildest imagination. In the shadow of a second, I decided, from the depths of my convictions, what to do. I told the doctor to take no action until after I had arrived and had a chance to pray over my father.

I was in the airport heading home, so it was easy to get back in the ticketing line and purchase a ticket to Georgia. I called my wife, Joy, and told her what was going on. I wanted to get a one-way ticket to go pray over my comatose father before I made the decision he had entrusted to me. She agreed with me, so I rechecked my bags and boarded a plane to fly to the small town where my father lived. I landed after ten at night, and the airport was deserted. No one was at the rental car counter and I did not want to call my father's cousin, so I jumped into a beat-up old taxi and asked the driver to take me to the veterans hospital. When I arrived, the waiting rooms were empty and the televisions were all turned off. The smell of antiseptic and burnt coffee hung in the air, and military paraphernalia decorated every wall. I carefully followed the color-coded painted lines on the ground until I found the intensive care station, where I asked a tired but friendly nurse where I could find Ernest Hill.

When she asked my name, I told her my first name, which is also Ernest. I had to swallow my anger as unforgiveness tried to rise in me even at that moment. Why would a man name a child after himself only to abandon him? This was the kind of question I would ask my father if the Lord allowed him to live. Questions like this had lived in my heart for many years—questions I had struggled to keep from festering into anger, rage, and unforgiveness.

The nurse directed me to his room. It was ultramodern and seemed out of place in comparison to the run-down wards and units I had walked through. The rest of the hospital seemed to be stuck in the late 1970s, but this unit looked like the sick bay on Star Trek. After consulting his lengthy chart, the nurse gave me an update on his condition. I placed my bags in the corner of the room and asked the nurse to excuse me for a few moments so I could pray. She said no words but just nodded and slipped from the room, leaving the door open. Lines and tubes seemed to stream from my father in every direction. Blips and beeps and the ever-present sound of a breathing machine filled the silence. My father did not move or speak. His eyes were shut as if he were sleeping peacefully. His hair was combed and clean, but his chin had slight stubble like a man who had missed a few days of shaving. I knelt beside his bed and, taking his hand, began to pray.

I asked the Lord to heal him. I asked Him to give him more time. I asked Him to give us more time together to answer some of the leftover questions of my childhood. I wanted time to try to build something from the wreckage his decisions had made in my life. I asked God not to give him the vengeance he deserved but instead to give him mercy. When I was a little boy, I had asked God to kill him more times than I can number. Now, as a mature man, I was asking God to let him live. I knew that in spite of the outcome, I had passed the test. I had overcome my own En Gedi. I had taken on this city, and it was one of the toughest challenges I had ever faced. This was not a battle with an external giant; this was a battle with myself.

Could I be so much like Jesus that I could forgive my own deadbeat father? I could. I did. So I prayed and cried that God would heal him. I prayed and cried that God would heal me. My father was in a coma, but I did not want my love and trust to also be comatose. I wanted to be totally healed and totally set free.

When I was done praying, I gathered my belongings, thanked the nurse, and headed down to the cabstand. The same cabbie was waiting for me, knowing that I would have no other way to get to my father's house than to call a taxi. My father's cousin had left a house key under the welcome mat for me, so I directed the taxi driver to that old one-level ranch house where my grandmother had been born and that my grandfather had rebuilt decades ago. The yellow porch light was on, and I found the key along with a note that had the four-digit code to disarm the alarm system my father had installed. When I looked at the code, I realized it was my birthdate. I set my bags down and wept, unable to walk into the house.

Finally, I pulled myself together and staggered into the house. I walked into my grandmother's room, still smelling of the super-sweet perfume she tended to overuse—and which I totally loved. I fell, fully dressed, onto the thick, flowery polyester comforter that covered her small bed and drifted into a dreamless sleep. I knew I was exhausted from the trip, but I was even more exhausted from experiencing the whirlwind of emotions over the last ten hours. I slept soundly until dawn and was awakened by the harsh sound of a phone ringing. My father still had the kinds of phones that plug into wall sockets and are connected to long cords that would reach across his little house. I snatched the mint-green receiver from the cradle and put the phone to my ear. It was the nurse calling for me. My father had woken up.

The ending had been rewritten, and God gave me three more years to get to know my father. For three years, I flew to Augusta to pay every bill, check medicines, and fight through the miles of red tape of the Veterans Administration. I went to serve meals, change dirty diapers, and give sponge baths. I went to hire and fire health care aides and make sure food was delivered three times a day. I went to watch baseball games on fuzzy hospital televisions, listening to the play-by-play on a speaker strapped to my father's hospital bed. I went to have three-hour-long conversations with a man I'd once hated but somehow learned to forgive, then to understand, and then to love. I went to change the ending of our story from one of anger and loss to one of peace in parting.

When I preached his funeral in a nearly empty room, my eulogy was short. I had said all the words I needed to say in those three years. The ending had been rewritten, and we did not part as enemies; we parted as friends.

This is what David did with Saul: he rewrote the ending from one of warfare to one of peace. Their encounter in En Gedi was the last time the two would see each other face-to-face. Their words were their final good-bye. David passed this test, this city. We all must pray that we can do the same.

10

ZIKLAG

The City of Discouragement

Some scholars believe that Ziklag was the original place the
Philistines conquered. It is possible that the seafaring invaders took
Ziklag from the tribe of Judah. David made a long journey, amass-
ing defeats and heartaches, before ending up in this city, which
compounded all this pain into major disappointment.

In 1 Samuel 26:25, we witness the last encounter David would
have with King Saul. Looking at this in hindsight, we get a glimpse
into the closing moments of the relationship between the king and
his son-in-law. David had just allowed King Saul to escape from
him a second time, and again he passed the test of revenge, elect-
ing to extend mercy to Saul. After this final encounter, Saul called
David his "son" and blessed him, declaring before all of David's
mighty men that David would go on to do great things and prevail
in everything. This was an amazing moment because God gave
David the gift of hearing his enemy speak a blessing over his life.

But in the very next verse, David pronounced that he believed
in his heart Saul would kill him one day. David was so unmoved
by Saul's words and gestures that he adopted a dangerous course

of action. He took his men into enemy territory to get farther away from Saul, and that decision nearly cost him his life. He did not return to the fortress of Judah, nor did he pack up and return to Bethlehem; David led his troops to Gath and formed a pseudo-alliance with one of the lords of the Philistines. You would think that after hearing Saul speak, David would have returned to his family's territory or tried to pursue a relationship with Saul. But he had been so disappointed by the actions of people he trusted that he was suffering from what I call a "dissipated heart." The words might be wonderful and the moment of reconciliation sweet, but it is possible to become so disappointed by the contradiction between people's words and their actions that trust is totally broken. David would not allow his heart to believe what his ears heard, because his spirit had been crushed too many times.

I have seen many people come to this place of pain—a place where people around them are trying to pour good things into their lives but they are unable to receive blessing because of past disappointment. Friendship becomes almost impossible because they are still wounded emotionally from past encounters. People are sometimes unable to embrace a new love opportunity because their hearts are still broken by previous relationships. Other people create hostile environments because they had been taken advantage of and are now resentful. At conferences around the globe in times of intense prayer, I have seen God heal the disappointed hearts of people. I have taught this chapter in meetings in which cries rise up from the audience as this point finds it's mark. The cries are so deep and painful that I have had to fight my desire to stop and join them at the altar to cry with them. The disappointed heart is a reality for so many people who have been let down and betrayed. They cannot connect in a new church because their hearts are still broken by what they went through at their last church. They cannot relax at a new job because of what they experienced in previous workplaces. They view their new situation through disillusioned eyes and cannot receive new information until there is heart reformation, so they find themselves like David: stuck in the disappointment of their pasts.

David was so burned by Saul that he could not allow himself to believe this blessing. He preferred to take his chances in enemy territory rather than be in any area under the rulership of Saul. David went to the city that produced Goliath and, bearing the sword of their fallen champion, directed his men into the mouth of the lion: the city of Gath itself.

Modern archaeologists have unearthed the gates to the city of Gath, and they are reputed to be the largest gates ever found in the nation of Israel. The uncovered walls were formidable, fortified, and well suited for the place that produced giants. Located halfway between Bethlehem and Askelon, the city reaches out to us from the ruins and reminds us of the reality of biblical history. These were real people who lived real lives and experienced real pain.

READY TO FIGHT

David elected to go to Gath because he knew it was enemy territory and was clear on what he was getting into there. He wouldn't face the possibility of being betrayed by his own people or having to kill any of them. In other words, David opted to be among known enemies rather than people who were supposed to be allies but could have turned on him. At least if everything went wrong, he could fight the Philistines in good conscience, which he could not do with his kinsmen.

What do you do when you love the people out to get you so much that you don't want to fight them? David was in this position, and this is a test we all will endure as we mature and progress in our walks toward our Jerusalems. We will be faced with foes who were once friends, and family who became enemies. We will endure pains and injuries from people we love far too much to hurt back.

Jesus loved people too much to hurt them, even when they were crucifying Him. His love for us kept Him from dealing with us according to our actions. The paralysis that comes when we are locked into loving relationships with hurtful people is difficult to break through. For David, the answer was to run to King Achish and to the city of Goliath.

STRANGE ALLIANCES

In looking at David's time in the Philistine territory, we see just how cunning he really was. This was probably the most duplicitous and double-dealing he had ever been in his young life. He pretended to be going out to do battle against the people of Judah, but he was really going to fight *with* them against the enemies of Israel. David loved his people far too much to raise his sword against them, even though he did not trust them.

David formed a strange alliance with King Achish and pretended to be his vassal. David brought some of the spoils of war to the Philistine king, acting as though he had taken these spoils from the children of Israel. This action, of course, caused the king to look upon David favorably. David brought more wealth to the king, who thought the warrior was fighting his enemy for him. Because Achish believed that David had switched allegiances, he put his trust and confidence in him. He allowed David and his six hundred mighty men to live close by. Only when David suggested that it might be inappropriate for him to be living in a royal city did Achish select a city for David and his men to occupy.

This time in the life of David teaches us that when we are suffering from disappointed hearts, we can be tempted to make unusual, maybe inappropriate, alliances with people we don't even like or trust. We can find ourselves entangled in relationships with people who normally would not merit our attention. We reach out to the wrong people and pretend to be like them in order to be accepted by them. Because we are misplaced, we have to live by deception and delusion to fit in. The trade-off is our real identity, and this is the real tragedy. Although David was doing no damage to Israel, he was doing damage to his own troops. His mighty men were not seeing a confident and courageous captain; they were seeing a devious leader who was not leading boldly. David was not an example of courage under pressure.

Situations like this reveal that we are actually afraid to trust God. We can become so jaded and hurt that even our trust in God is under attack. When we resort to living by our own cunning and attempt to fit in with people we don't belong with—when we lose our personal identity and authenticity—it is a chief indicator that we are not living by faith.

Whenever we decide to live by our own wits, we will end up at our wit's end. It requires too much energy to try to be who we are not. The unintended consequence of this choice is that the people who have known us the longest lose touch with who we are. We are pretending to be someone they would not have committed to or connected with initially. This identity confusion causes even the people who know us and love us to question who we are.

THE WRONG DIRECTION

Strangely, David had the priest with the ephod with him, but he did not seek the Lord's counsel for the critical decision of going to Achish. David did not reach out to God, nor did he ask the priest to intercede or beseech the Lord for direction. David just let his heart dictate how he would act, without any outside deliberation or godly input. When our hearts are so broken that we no longer trust godly or biblical counsel, we are in trouble. Mired in our own emotions and locked within our distorted mind-sets, we are hindered from hearing any outside voices. We don't even seek to hear from the people who are hearing from God. The challenges we face require that we hear from God, but when we are in those broken places, there is a tendency to close down our ability to hear.

I have watched people stop listening many times, and the results are always devastating in the long run. We need God's direction so we can be sure we are walking in His perfect will. We don't know that David was supposed to be in the territory of the Philistines or that he was to be in the service of Achish. Maybe he moved in the wrong direction by going to Gath. It is quite possible that he would have been safe in Israel. But even though David made this decision without God's input, God was able to turn it for David's good.

When we go in the wrong direction and pick the unsuitable path, the peace and clarity we need to progress to the next level is cut off from us. When we refuse to seek God's guidance before acting, He allows us to move in the way we think is best, leaving us to our own devices. Praise God, He does not abandon us when we have decided to go out on our own. Praise God, He is still with us even when, like David, we allow our disappointment with people to infect and affect our ability to trust in Him.

The prophet Jonah wandered from the prescribed path, but God did not abandon him to the seas. He sent a big fish to retrieve him from the deep and then transport and deposit him in the place God had intended him to be in the first place. God won't allow us to go too far in the wrong direction. He will lovingly correct our course if we are willing to listen to Him. Certainly Jonah, after he was vomited out of the belly of the big fish, could have decided not to preach in Nineveh, but he had a complete change of heart.

The storms God allows to come upon us as a result of our disobedience or lack of trust should send us back in the right direction if we are humble enough to hear and heed His voice. Either as a whisper in a cave or as a wail of the storm, God will correct our course; we just have to be willing to be corrected.

It is a daunting thought to consider the possibility that this entire season David spent in the Philistine territory was unnecessary—that perhaps Saul's blessing was legitimate. David could have been reunited with his wife, his friend Jonathan, and all his possessions earlier had he only been able to receive the blessing. This is a hard thought for most of us, because we have to then examine our own lives. We must ask the difficult question of whether we have delayed our deliverance or prolonged our problems because we have not received the freedom that God offered us. We have to wrestle with this question so we can adjust to the new information when God makes a way of escape for us. What if David had believed Saul? What if he had never gone into Philistine territory? Not all "what if" questions are useful, but in this case they help us reach our truest potential. Each time we miss the mark, asking this teaches us to trust God more. It hones our ability to hear His voice and causes us to press our ears closer to His heart. Then we can discern the heartbeat of God for our lives. Contemplating lost seasons of our lives is hard, but it is one of the best ways to ensure we do not wander out of God's intended territory again.

David prayed before he attacked Keilah, and he sought God before leaving, but he entered the enemy's territory and never sought the Lord once. This journey in the wrong direction would cost him, but he survived because when God has a plan for someone's life, even missteps and mistakes work out for the individual's good (Rom. 8:28).

THE ENEMY'S GIFT

David's cunning had so fooled Achish into accepting him and his soldiers that he awarded David the empty city of Ziklag. Why Ziklag was abandoned and then given to Achish are lost to history. All we know from Scripture is that the city was within the authority of Achish to give and that it was not occupied at that time. David and his mighty men, along with their families, entered this city and lived there for almost a year and a half. They built homes, planted crops, grazed their cattle, and dug wells. Their wives and children no longer had to live in a forest or make camp in the rocky caves. They had houses, fields, and safety, even in enemy territory.

When David and his men pretended to go out to fight the Israelites, they laid waste to the enemies of Israel: the Geshurites, Gezrites, and Amalekites. When Achish asked David who he fought with that day, he would tell him he fought with Judah, his own family, such as the Jerahmeelites, or with the Kenites, who were the tribe from which Moses's father-in-law descended.

David ran this ruse for sixteen months without detection. It seemed that as long as he delivered spoils to King Achish, everything was great. Achish did not investigate David's claims about whom he was attacking, and David was careful to eliminate all traces of where the spoils were coming from. This deal seemed to be working, as David moved forward and had a city of his own. The borders of the Philistine lands were safe from the invasion of Saul, and everything David had been looking for was being supplied in enemy territory. Their collective coffers were filled with enemy goods. The livestock and expensive raiment were spread throughout the city, the visible evidence of a bloodied and successful band of raiders. They were scamming the Philistines and avoiding King Saul. However, they were surrounded by the heathens who were their sworn rivals. They did not spill the blood of their fellow Israelites, but they were merrily warming their hands at the fires of the enemy. Soon they would be expected to join King Achish's army in a final battle with King Saul's forces.

This territory was a gift from the enemy king. It wasn't ground that was earned in hard-fought battle, nor was it ground purchased with money. Because of that, David and his men found an uneasy rest in this city that was situated in the territory God gave to the tribe of Judah—territory that was already theirs but had been taken by the Philistines. Seen in this light, it was an insult to give a son of Judah a place that belonged to him in the first place. This is like a squatter giving us the keys back to our own home and making us pay him rent for the privilege. When we remember who David was destined to be—the future king of Israel—it is even more insulting that he was being given territory by an enemy king.

By receiving enemy territory, David became a tenant, with limited rights, when God intended him to reign supreme in this territory and both hold and extend the kingdom. Being given enemy territory ran counter to God's call on his life. He was not born to be given ground; he was born to take enemy territory. This city was a place David was not supposed to be in. Still, he learned this lesson so well that later he did not allow even one of his men to give him a plot of land upon which to build the temple of God (2 Sam. 24:24).

THE FOSTER HOME

The day came for my sister and me to be taken by the social worker to our foster home. It was a day filled with painful emotions. As the social worker drove us the four miles, Marie was awash in a puddle of tears. She had never been on her own, having run from my mother's house straight to our grandparents' house. She had never spent a day away from our family members. Perhaps this is what made going to the foster home more traumatic for her. She cried all the way there as well as the entire first day and night we were in the home. She was inconsolable, and I didn't have the words to comfort her. I was, however, being as charming and affable as I could. My defense was to find a way to fit in, mask my own emotions, and win over my new foster family. The house was large and seemed to be filled with bedrooms. It had a side yard and a chain-link fence.

My new foster mother was strong with a kind face. Though not a churchgoer, she seemed to have an open, giving heart. I was not afraid in her presence. On that first day, however, I tried to learn the maze of the house and map out exit routes should Marie and I need to escape. The home came with a foster grandfather and two foster sisters, one of whom was nearly an adult and the other a few years older than me. I tried to learn everyone's names as quickly as possible as well as the house rules, such as who was in charge and what the dynamics of this new situation were. And I soon realized I was living in enemy territory.

This family did not attend church. They stayed home on Sundays and lived a lifestyle so antithetical to the "holiness" tradition I knew that I barely had a clue how to view them. They were kind to take us in, but they were not Christians as I knew Christians to be. They did not sing the songs of Zion, nor did they speak the language of the church. They were not immoral people, but for a boy who went to church almost six days of the week and loved it, I felt I was living among pagans. They lived a

life that was filled with sin and did so seemingly without thought
of repentance or bothered conscience. I was so busy trying to fit
in and not highlight how different I was from them that I never
corrected them or confronted them on their life practices. I just
saw them as sinners—nice sinners, but sinners nonetheless.

The foster home was a blessing to us because it provided food
and shelter, but it was not our home. We were always outsiders
and felt like intruders in their tight family system. Because our
own family system, with all its supposed moral superiority, was
so fractured, we didn't dare criticize theirs. I was eight years old
and my sister was ten, and we were living with strangers. For the
first time, I heard profanity, witnessed illicit drug use, saw female
nudity and pornography, and learned about teenage and premari-
tal sex. I was exposed to non-Christian religions and secular music.
I learned that there were people who did not view God the way I
was raised to see Him. I was never mistreated, but my innocence
was assaulted. My childlike Christian worldview was challenged
and my heart questioned which way to turn. The young preacher
in me wanted to rail against these practices, just like the hellfire
revivalist who visited the little church where I spent my summers,
but I remained silent.

I kept my calling to myself, because I didn't think my foster
family would understand or support my desire to enter the ministry. I tried to fly below the radar, to speak and act like the other
kids in the house and neighborhood. I realized early on that to be
holy around these kids was to be a square or sucker. I needed to
be able to use profanity easily and know all the secular songs and
dances. I had to be willing to fight even though I had been taught

to turn the other cheek. I learned not to look shocked when people did things I found shocking. I had to hide my innocence.

I had no big brother or father to rescue me. If I found myself surrounded by bullies or if I was discovered to be an outsider, I really was in trouble. I learned to flatter my adversaries and mirror the morals of the people around me. In short, I learned how to hide in plain sight. But inside I always knew that if I stayed in this house too long, I might lose my own way and be swallowed up in a lifestyle I was not called to live. Now I longed to be reunited with my mother and returned to the sanctity of the church.

I would pray when I was alone. I spent many hours walking their family dog, Skipper, a black Labrador retriever. On those long walks through the neighborhood, I would pray aloud. I would wonder to God how I would ever reach my Jerusalem being raised in this environment. I asked Him how I would fulfill my ministry calling—the one I knew was upon my life—now that we did not even attend a church. I wondered how I would learn to preach while I was living in this strange land. I asked God how this could be good for me, and at the time He did not answer. I see now that this experience softened my heart toward people who live outside the moral umbrella of the church I was raised in. I learned that a person doesn't necessarily have to sit in pews or sing from hymnbooks to be a decent person. I learned to look beyond people's behaviors to see them for who they are at heart. I learned to reject the hellfire-and-brimstone quick judgments of the preaching tradition I was raised in.

Most important, I learned that I wanted to go home, to be with my mother. I prayed that my mother, who was working hard to fulfill everything the courts required to get us back, would be successful. I prayed that I could return to the church and to the path of my destiny. I knew that through some bad decision making by the adults in my life and through the complete dereliction by my deadbeat father, my sister and I had been placed into a home that was so far from our true destinies that we needed to get out of there as quickly as the authorities would allow.

THE MISFIT

David did not fit in. King Achish invited him to join him and his troops in a great battle. This was not like the small skirmishes the mighty men had been conducting against the Amalekites or the Gezrites; this was to be a massive battle between a joint army of the lords of the Philistines and the combined armies of the tribes of Israel. Achish called David and his mighty men to come out of their homes in Ziklag and commanded them to march for three days to the city of Aphek, where the Philistines had amassed. They had such great numbers and King Saul was so frightened that he consulted a witch for a prediction of the outcome. Because the heavens were closed to him, Saul consulted hell. He was informed that this battle would be his last.

King Achish was forcing David to publicly declare his allegiance to the Philistines. David had to fight against the forces of Israel, and there appeared to be no way to avoid it. But other Philistine kings also had heard of the exploits of the warrior David and the songs the women of Israel sang about him, so the other kings of the Philistines were unwilling to have David or his troops among their ranks while fighting the Israelites. They demanded that he be sent home and quit the field of battle. God made a way of escape for David so he would not have to fight against Saul. Even though David had aligned himself with the Philistines, God made it possible for him to avoid having the blood of his countrymen on his hands. God is so gracious that even though David had gone in the wrong direction, there was a way of escape. His grace still shelters us when we are operating in a prayerless position, even when we have made decisions without consulting Him. To kill Saul or fight the host of Israel would have disqualified David from being the king. So although God allowed David to exercise his free will, He still managed to salvage his destiny.

David and his mighty men were forced to turn around and make the three-day trek back to their home base in Ziklag. On their way, they looked up and saw a plume of black smoke rising in the sky. Appearing like dark paint splashed across the canvas of the horizon, the smoke filled their hearts with fear. The acrid smell of a burned city hung in the air. The mighty men hastened their marching for fear the smoke was rising from the place they had left their wives and children three days earlier.

Can you imagine their faces as their march home turned into an open run? Can you picture their hands as they white-knuckled their bridles, urging their beasts to move fast across the open field? Can you envision their hearts in their throats and their stomachs boiling with acid? They must have been afraid to see the worst but unable to turn away. The charred walls of the city were still smoking when they finally arrived. The city was deserted, and all they fought so hard to gain was gone. They expected to see the bright

eyes of their children and be met by the thankful embraces of their
wives. Instead, they encountered only emptiness and loss. All their
sons, daughters, and wives were gone. Both of David's wives had
been taken, and no one knew whether their loved ones were alive.

The men of David, his mighty men, began to weep. For the
previous sixteen months, they had been obliterating the towns of
Israel's enemies. They had taken no prisoners, killing every man,
woman, and child for fear that one would escape and bring word
to King Achish that David was not raiding the towns of his own
people but pillaging the cities of the Canaanites. For more than
a year, they had been doing to others what they now feared had
been done to them. They did not know if their wives had been
raped and their children sacrificed. All they knew was that they
were gone. They did not know that the Amalekites carried all their
family members away alive, so they fell into the dust and wept with
loud screams of despair.

These brave men fell headlong into the ashes of their own
homes, sorting through the debris looking for the charred corpses of
the people they loved. Scripture says that they cried until they could
cry no more. They wept until they had no more tears to weep, and
then their grief turned into anger. Seeking someone to blame, they
turned to David with bloodshot eyes and began to discuss killing
him (1 Sam. 30).

In 1 Chronicles 12:18, we read that the mighty men went to
Ziklag with words of "peace, peace," but now we find that the same
mighty men were ready to hurl stones at David until he fell dead.
The mighty men who first met David in the cave of Adullam had
lost their loyalty to David in the city of Ziklag. The same broken

men who rallied to David and made him their captain when they were distressed, indebted, and discontent were now his judges and executioners. They deliberated together on whether they should rebel against David and put him to death in the streets of the burning city.

This was the reality of Ziklag. In your city of Ziklag, you will face total abandonment by allies. All your possessions might be taken from you, and you might feel as though your whole life is going up in flames. In Ziklag, you might feel isolated and alone because even the people who should believe in you have turned away. You might weep until your eyes can make no more tears. You might cry out but receive no pity and no human compassion. You might feel you have been stripped down to nothing. Ziklag was one of the lowest moments in the course of young David's life: no wife, no children, no money, no cattle, no house, and no allies. David had nothing left in Ziklag but God.

When you realize you have nothing left but God, you cannot help but become encouraged if you really know who God is. David found his source of encouragement only in the Lord, his God. The word for encouragement in the Hebrew is *chazaq*, and it means to "fasten upon." So David fastened himself upon the Lord. He hung his life, hope, and confidence upon the Lord. He tied his future to Him. Then he called for the priest and the ephod, and for the first time in this season and city of his life, he prayed. David sought God for direction, because it could not be found anywhere else.

David's grand schemes and great cunning were not enough to lead him out of this situation. He was done making decisions without first seeking godly counsel. He realized that even though he had been moving in the wrong direction, living in the wrong city, and doing the wrong thing, the grace of God was still available to him. This was one of David's strengths that he displayed throughout his life: he knew how to repent. David would not be marked as a perfect man but as a man of perfect repentance.

David teaches us what to do when our world seems to be burning down around us and every relationship has ceased to be reliable. In our own Ziklags, we have to fasten ourselves to the Lord. The total abandonment of man teaches us the all-sufficient power of our God. Our Ziklags teach us that grace is always available to the truly repentant and that God can turn the worst situation around. Encouragement comes from discovering that if God is all we have, then He is all we need. Prayer is the privilege of the penitent, and God does not abandon His children behind enemy lines.

David finally sought the Lord for direction, and God answered him quickly. God told him to pursue his enemy. He assured him that he would not only find the Amalekites but also "recover all" (1 Sam. 30:8). David was told that they would recover all their family members, friends, and stolen possessions. With the assurance of the ephod, the confidence of David's mighty men was restored and David was able to regain control of them. They did indeed find the Amalekites, take back their families, and secure the restoration of all that was taken from Ziklag. They also seized all the bounty the raiders had taken during their invasion of the south of Israel. David recovered not just his "all" but all the spoils taken from Israel as well.

This is how God works in our lives as well, redeeming for us what we lose in Ziklag. He restores to us more than what we lost. He repairs our faith, redeems our time, and rebuilds our confidence. Ziklag is the place where God changes our losses into wins and uses our bad situations to miraculously position us for good. Ziklag becomes a place of blessing. What we thought would destroy us, God uses to make us better.

THE REUNION

For three long years, my sister and I lived in the foster home, cut off from our family and removed from our faith. All the while, my mother wound her way through the red tape of the court system, desperately trying to bring our family back together.

Over time, we were allowed to have weekly phone calls with her, and through this I began to see my mother—the mother of my childhood—reappear before my eyes. And then I started to pray in earnest that our little war-torn family would be restored.

My mother worked tirelessly trying to prove to the courts that she was able once again to shoulder the responsibility of caring for and raising her two children on her own. She was brave and fearless as she stood before the judgmental eyes of people who did not understand her struggle. And I never felt more proud of her. She attended counseling. She secured employment. She creatively decorated and furnished our one-bedroom apartment, making it possible for the social worker to approve our residence. She turned that one bedroom into two with milk crates she covered in wallpaper so my sister could have her privacy and I could have mine. She made her bed on a couch while making sure we would have warm beds to sleep in. She even started going back to our old church. She had our love, but she also slowly restored our confidence in her as a mother. Eventually, we met with her monthly for supervised visits.

The one-bedroom apartment was so much smaller than the foster home. There was no backyard to play in and no dog to teach new tricks. Still, home was where my mother was. Before her depression and her abuse of us, home meant being in a place where Christianity was real and relational. Home was where my moral compass was biblically supported and aligned. Each year my mother applied for our family to be reunited, but each time the courts said no. They ran us through a gauntlet of social workers and therapists trying to determine if we really wanted to live with our mother. The answer was always yes. Love learns to forgive, love learns how to heal, and God is Love. He gave me the strength to forgive my mother and find a way to love her, even after all that had transpired.

I was eleven years old when the social worker drove my sister and me the four miles to my mother's apartment, our little suitcases stuffed with clothes. We climbed the tenement stairs that stank with the smell of stale urine from the drug addicts and alcoholics who stood guard on the steps each day. We walked down the dark hallway to her door. I knocked and heard the metal lock slide to the right, and as the door opened, there stood my mother with tears running down her face. She took Marie and me into her arms, and we were all finally home.

11

HEBRON

The City of Almost There

Hebron is one of the most ancient cities in all of Israel. Many scholars date its founding back to the year 1727 BC, so this city was hundreds of years old when David arrived there with his mighty men. But David was not the first or even the foremost biblical character to sojourn there.

The Bible first mentions Hebron in connection with the patriarch Abraham, David's forefather. In Hebron, Abraham (then still called Abram) finished his walking inspection of the land God had promised him after he separated from his nephew Lot. It was in Hebron that he pitched his tent and built an altar unto the Lord (Gen. 13). Later, his wife, Sarah, died in Hebron, and he purchased the cave of Machpelah and the ground that stood before it so he could put his bride into that ground forever.

This was the first time the burial of a person was recorded in the Bible. This was also the first plot of land Abraham purchased and therefore the first he rightfully owned in the land he was promised by the Lord. He had built altars before in the Promised Land but never on territory he owned. Hebron represents a significant first step: it is the first step to seeing the total fulfillment of the promise of God. The Hittites had occupied and owned the land first, but Abraham respectfully bought it from them. The Canaanites were more than willing to give Abraham his choice from the best of their tombs, but he gracefully refused. He requested instead that they entreat the owner of the cave to see if he would be willing to sell it to Abraham. Once the owner of the cave was told Abraham wanted it, he offered to just give the cave and the grounds around it to Abraham. But once again, Abraham declined. He was unwilling to allow the first ground he owned in the Promised Land to be given to him. He insisted on purchasing it.

In Hebron, Abraham was not a sojourner anymore; he was a landowner. Even though he bargained with God over how many good men would need to be found in Sodom and Gomorrah, he did not dicker over the price of the cave (Gen. 23). He paid full price and did so quickly, because this was his first real step into experiencing the promise God gave him. His sons Isaac and Ishmael later buried him in that cave right next to his first wife, and they still lie there to this day.

Hebron is considered the second-most holy city in Judaism today, exceeded only by Jerusalem. But in the days of David, Jerusalem was still in the hands of the Canaanites, and the tabernacle or temple had yet to be established there. It was in Hebron that David went to set up his kingdom in Judah. He started his own invasion into the territories of Israel—his own march toward the fulfillment of God's promise for his life. Hebron would not be the final place where he would fulfill his divine purpose, but it was the staging area for his long-awaited march into Jerusalem. It was the final base camp on his arduous and dangerous ascent to the heights of Zion. In this sense, Hebron was to David as it was to Abraham: the initial point of owning his purpose, the place where he realized he was "almost there."

God has a way of turning things around after we finally decide to reach out to Him for divine help and guidance. David was able to leave Ziklag after an amazing victory. Not only did God empower him to recover his own family but he also recovered the family members of his mighty men. He did indeed recover his "all." What's more, the "all" God was referring to was far greater than what David had imagined. He collected enough for himself, plus there was enough to be divided among his troops, including those who did not even fight. The bounty was even great enough that David sent a portion to the elders of Judah in Bethel, Ramoth, Jattir, Aroer, Siphmoth, Eshtemoa, Rachal, the cities of the Jerahmeelites and Kenites, Hormah, Chorashan, and Athach (1 Sam. 30:26–31). He did this because he intended to leave the territory of the Philistines and return to Israel, believing he had learned all God intended for him there. He used a portion of the "all" he recovered to secure for himself and his men an all-access pass to the territory of Judah.

While David was still in the burned city of Ziklag, a messenger came from the battlefield bringing grim news from Mount Gilboa: Israel had suffered a terrible defeat, and Saul had died in battle. Additionally, David learned that Jonathan and two of his brothers had been killed. David mourned their losses because he loved these people, but the death of Saul at the hands of the Philistines was part of the fulfillment of God's plan to restore David's "all."

Saul's death left the kingdom in disarray. Abner, the captain of Saul's army, saw to it that Ishbosheth, Saul's remaining son, was placed upon his father's throne (2 Sam. 2:8–9). This was only a military appointment, and the kings of Israel were not decided by generals but by God. Ishbosheth reigned for two short years. The kingdom was divided because the tribe of Judah rejected Ishbosheth and made David their king.

Although the news of Saul's death brought David sadness, it was a signal that the prophecy he received at Ziklag was absolutely true and so much larger than he could have imagined. His "all" included the fulfillment of the promise he had received from Samuel back in Bethlehem. This marked the turning point in David's life, as four of the five men who had a claim to the throne died at the battle of Mount Gilboa. Just one person had a stronger claim to the throne, but it was clear to David, his mighty men, and eventually the people of Judah that God was orchestrating the circumstances to bring David to the throne.

Ziklag was a city of swirling emotions for David. It is dizzying to see him move from deep discouragement over the loss of his family to the sheer joy he must have felt when he marched his family home. Then we see him rejoice at the abundance of gifts he was able to send to the elders of Israel and shed tears again when he heard that his father-in-law and his covenant brother were both dead. As David marched away from the burned-down city of Ziklag, he did so rejoicing over what had been restored to him while grieving over what he had lost. It was a bittersweet departure. He did not return to the city of Bethlehem, because he had already passed that test. This time he went to Hebron.

SURVIVING "SAUL SITUATIONS"

Imagine if the thing that threatened you the most—the enemy who plagued your thoughts nights and day—was suddenly removed from your life. Wouldn't it be an incredibly freeing moment? David did not wish Saul ill, but nonetheless the removal of the assassin made him free. Saul's death was a bitter pill to swallow for David, but this pill was also quite medicinal.

David could return to Judah, but he was a different man from who he was when he left. His journey through the many cities prepared him for a greater role of service. He was no longer the shepherd boy delivering his father's pledge to the armies of Israel; he was a mighty captain of an experienced army. He had acquired great wealth through his victories in battle and was the preferred leader of Israel. This was how he entered Hebron. It was not the sad and scared processional of a wanted man being chased by a demonized king; this was the triumphant return of a would-be king.

Imagine if your "Saul" were dead—if your situation were over and ended—and for the first time in years you could allow yourself to exhale and breathe the fresh air of freedom. Your own Hebron is where you experience the freedom that comes from having the greatest and longest enemy of your peace finally removed. I call this "the death of your Saul." Goliath threatened Israel for forty days at Elah but threatened David for no more than one day. Goliath was the most famous enemy David defeated, but the struggle with the giant was not long lived. Most scholars estimate that David spent four years running from

Saul. Sometimes it is the struggles no one really knows about that shape us into the people God intends us to be. It is these longer struggles that crystallize our faith and refine our beliefs. "Saul situations" aren't fixed overnight, nor do they disappear with one prayer; they forge your faith by teaching you how to rely on God.

Saul situations can last many seasons, ignoring calendars and time lines because they are completely in the hands of God. Only He can determine when the situations have produced the character, skills, principles, and resolve He needs us to learn. We are not allowed to be the judge of this process, nor are we allowed to determine when it should end. Only God can call an end to a Saul situation, and we have to trust that He is in control. The death of your Saul signals the end of one season of challenge and the beginning of your entry into your next city. Your destiny is secure, your purpose providently set, and no Saul can stop what God has planned for your life.

Your Hebron is the place where you realize you are almost there and are finally facing the right direction. When you reach your Hebron, you will have made that critical course correction, and the sadness of your past city will begin to fade. You will be full of the experience and wisdom you have garnered on your journey and will learn the final lessons needed to move into your divine assignment. Your divine purpose is before you, and you are heading toward the fulfillment of God's promise for your life. Your own doubts and even the doubts of your enemies cease to find a root in your heart. You know who you are and who you are becoming.

DEFINING RELATIONSHIPS

Hebron in Hebrew means the "seat of association," and in your Hebron you will begin to make key connections with people who will usher you into your next city. This is where the associations critical to your divine purpose are established and fostered. Hebron is so close to Jerusalem that it can easily be overlooked, but it is where you will discover relationships you will need for the rest of your life. The miracle of walking into your divine purpose will always be accomplished within the context of relationships. The kingdom of God always advances in the company of others.

During Jesus's ministry, He called the disciples to Himself, but always when they were together. He also trained them together and sent them to do ministry together. When Jesus was resurrected, He met His disciples when they were together. Where two or three of them were gathered together in His name, He was in their midst (Matt. 18:20). The emphasis on the togetherness of the ministry and training of His disciples is a sign that Jesus is interested in our developing purposeful relationships.

In a society that celebrates and congratulates rugged individualism, it is important to note just how much the Scriptures and particularly the ministry of Jesus Christ celebrate relationship. Friendship is the coin of the realm, and relationship is the most important thing in the kingdom. There is power that comes to us when we are serving together—an anointing that comes to us in our unity. This anointing was necessary for the disciples of Jesus and was necessary for the preparation of David before he could advance to his Jerusalem. We cannot fully become who we are to be until we are in covenant with the right people: people who understand who we are now and who we are to be. They realize God has an established purpose for our lives and are willing to align themselves with us.

The disciples of Jesus were called together and served together to touch the world. Likewise, David's call to be king could not be fulfilled in isolation. One cannot be a king without a nation, nor can someone be a leader without a group of people to lead. Without a vision the people would perish, but without a people the vision also will die. The fullness of David's call to lead presupposed the people of Israel would agree to faithfully follow his leadership. David could not live out his God-ordained purpose without there being an "association"—a seat of agreement—surrounding him. In Jerusalem, David would gain rulership over all twelve tribes of Israel, but in Hebron, he gained rulership over one: Judah. It was the first installment of what he would one day oversee. It was the preparatory class for the authority and responsibility he would eventually have. In Hebron, David operated and led in a smaller setting. This city was the tithe God entrusted to him at the first to prepare him for the whole.

When God moves you into your Hebron, He will give you a portion to be responsible for before He fully entrusts you with everything you are to have. I often meet people who want to run right past their Hebron to get to their Jerusalem, but this is a mistake. We must not despise a small beginning, because God uses the smallest things to prepare us for the great. The strongest man is still born a baby. The tallest oak is hidden in the heart of the tiny acorn. God starts on the seed level so the dream can fully develop and we will not be overwhelmed by the harvest. Hebron was David's place of dominion in seed form. He had dominion over Hebron in association with the elders of Judah first so he could learn the lessons that would come only from walking in a measure of authority.

God may require you to clean the kitchen before you are allowed to take over the restaurant. He may require you to assist the teacher before He allows you to be head of the class. Like Ruth, you may have to glean in the fields of Bethlehem before you can own the entire barley field. The process may seem slow and arduous, but the payoff is beyond your wildest dreams. The pain of preparation cannot be compared to the joy of obtaining your goal. When people coalesce around the vision God has given you, that is the time to get excited, because you are on the right road for reaching your place of promise.

LIVING IN THE PLACE OF "ALMOST THERE"

There are seasons of your life when you are almost there—stages when you are so close to your goal that you can almost see and taste the reward. In these seasons of your life, the excitement is almost palpable. Your heart beats like a bass drum in your chest. In spite of all you have gone through, you are so close! When you are living in that place, you must start healing from what you have gone through. You have enough outward evidence that your promise is coming toward you that you can begin to be optimistic about your life. The pain of what you endured is real, so God gives you the time to heal from it. The rejection and dejection you have experienced in other cities can scar your psyche. If you do not have a season to heal, you can end up bringing a damaged "you" into a prepared promise.

The promise is perfected, so we must also be perfected before we can enter into it. A premature entry into your personal Jerusalem can cause you to drag your past pains into your future. Yesterday's pain has no place in tomorrow's promise. God detoxes you in Hebron before bringing you into your Jerusalem. But you have to trust Him to do His work in you first so you don't contaminate your potential. In the "almost there" position, your shoulders adjust to the weight of responsibility, your heart opens up to care for a greater number of people, and your mind develops the capacity to deal with the details necessary to lead, assist, and direct a larger organization.

"Almost there" can be exciting but quite challenging at the same time. We are expected to meet and lead new people. The road David walked was long and hard, but in Hebron, he was finally crowned the king of Judah. He was not just leading one city; he was dealing with all the towns of Judah. He was giving leadership to the elders of those towns and was responsible for all the people in them. The failure of his leadership in Ziklag was being healed by his subsequent success in Judah. This leadership experience was critical because in just a few years, the tremendous weight of leading an entire nation would fall upon his shoulders. He would have to interact with and lead the elders of every tribe. He would have to raise an army and confront the Philistines who routed and defeated Saul's army. He would have to reconstitute a government and a broken nation. All these tools and tactics were first developed in Hebron. This "almost" space was just the beginning, but "almost there" was really a gift. God gives us chances to practice in the realms familiar to us before He propels us into places that are promised yet untested. Be careful not to rush through the place of "almost there," because God is doing a great work in your life.

RECALLED

When I was fifteen years old and had been back home with my mother for a year, the men of my mother's church planned a ministry trip to the Bronx. I was adjusting to living in our little apartment with my mother. I had not had much direction for so long and had become so self-sufficient that having a real parent to oversee and protect me was a foreign concept. I had to adjust to asking permission to do things and having someone check my homework, monitor my grooming habits, and regulate my television time. At the same time, I was readjusting to living in a Christian home again. No longer did the stereo blare out R & B music. That was replaced with the sounds of Maranatha Music and Andraé Crouch. No longer did the pungent odor of marijuana poorly covered by the sweet smell of incense slide under closed doors. It was replaced by the smell of apple crisp and fried chicken. I was home: back to the ordered and clean home I had before my family was broken apart.

I was changed, though. I was not the outgoing child I had been. I had laid aside my dreams of preaching and traveling. I lived each day looking for calamity to strike. I saved each cent as though it would be my last. I didn't allow myself to dream about tomorrow, because I was always expecting the world to turn upside down. I liked the men of the church, but I did not trust them. I could speak to them and be friendly, but I stared at them from the other side of emotional walls. These walls I had built to make sure the loss of another adult relationship would not shatter my world. I loved my mother, but I did not trust her. It would be many years before I would feel safe enough to share my heart with anyone. I hid my stick in the closet and saved my pennies until they were dollars, always ready to slide out the window and run.

My mother strongly suggested I go on the trip with the church-men, and I went out of obedience. I had never been to New York City or even wanted to go, but I climbed into the back of a church van and headed out on the first ministry road trip of my life. We went to see a bus ministry transporting thousands of children in the Bronx. Each Saturday they knocked on doors in the tenements and invited kids to come onto school buses and ride with them to a service designed just for children. The children's workers sang silly worship songs with the children at first. Then after everyone was warmed up, they began to lead them into slow, intimate worship songs. These songs caused the kids to look up into heaven and almost see the smiling face of Father God.

Then the leader took the stage. He was a tall, thin white man with a shaggy, pageboy hairdo. His voice sounded as though he had been gargling glass for an hour, as he had preached hard and loud to children for so many years. He didn't wear a suit like the pastors I was used to seeing; he wore dingy blue jeans and a brown T-shirt with a picture of Yogi Bear on the front. But when he began to preach to the children about a God who loved them enough to give His life for them, I felt something shift in the room.

He preached in this packed building as the children sat on bleachers or filled folding chairs that seemed to cover every inch of the floor. As this man preached, I felt as though I heard the voice of God. A shift began in the part of me that had forgiven my father but could never trust a man and that loved my mother but didn't know if she could lead our family.

The man was Rev. Bill Wilson. When this skinny man, born in my hometown of Boston, started preaching, something came alive again in my spirit. It was not that I had not heard preaching; the pastors in my mother's church preached every week. But this man spoke in a way that gripped my heart. He had been abandoned by his parents as a child and had been taken into the kind home of a Christian stranger. Somehow he met and had been adopted spiritually by a great and world-famous preacher. Rev. Wilson had been sent by his home church into the Bronx to minister life and hope to a rejected and lost generation.

The backdrop of his sermons was the burned-out, bombed-out buildings that stood like broken teeth along the trash-strewn streets even the police refused to walk alone. The crack-infested neighborhood stood behind him as he preached, and I still could hear the voice of God. I saw a glimpse again of what I would do. I felt again the foreshadowing of a future I could not even imagine or describe. I believed in a future I lacked the vocabulary to explain and had not one role model to point to—except this man, who stood on a makeshift stage in front of three thousand children. Somehow I realized that even though it felt a million miles away, I just might be closer to my Jerusalem than I thought.

The emotional walls I had built were not all completely shat-
tered in that moment, but that part of me I thought was dead
could finally see light coming through small cracks. As Rev. Wilson
preached, my dreams came back. In the story of his past, I saw my
future, and though we never met until many years later, I knew
that his message that day was just for me.

That very night, the entire men's group slept on the floor of
the gym, but I did not sleep a wink. While the men were talking
about going back to Boston and launching a children's bus ministry similar to this one, I knew I would somehow have to help
them, because this would be part of my destiny and my healing. I
had just entered my Hebron.

When we returned to Boston, I instantly joined this new ministry in my mother's church. I was too young to drive the bus, but
I quickly learned to be outgoing, vocal, and bold enough to walk
through the hallways of Boston's most dangerous housing projects, knocking on strangers' doors to ask the parents if they would
allow our team to take their kids to church on Saturdays. I learned
how to speak to people with confidence and clarity. I learned how
to knock on new doors each week and meet new people. I also
learned how to lead children onto the bus from all over the projects
and check and recheck my clipboard each time to make sure each
child was safe and accounted for.

I learned how to sing silly songs with the children, but I also
learned how to lead them into times of worship when we felt
God's presence filling our little chapel. Somehow in the midst of
my leading and caring for these children, I began to heal. It was as
if by watching them just be children, I regained those lost years of

my own childhood. As I helped usher them into the presence of a loving God to be healed, I also was healed. My confidence was being restored, my faith was being rebuilt, and as I taught them the stories of Jesus, I found I still had a voice.

Almost thirty years later, I would return to the Bronx and visit that same children's chapel. I would shake Rev. Wilson's hand and tell him that a young, broken boy heard him preach one day and God used his preaching to help restore that boy's dream. This time I was with two of the children's pastors who serve on our church staff in Denver. I did not have to sleep on the floor of their gym, but that night, as I had a late coffee with my coworkers, we could barely sleep for dreaming together about what a bus ministry could look like in our city.

THE WIVES OF HEBRON

Hebron for David truly became a seat of association beyond the relationships he established with elders. He also brought his wives there and took more wives, establishing his royal family. The names of these wives give us a clear indication of what God wants to add to our lives when we are in our Hebron. They give us insight into what has to be restored in us before we are ready to move forward.

Abigail

Her name means "my Father's joy." In Hebron, God wants us to begin to experience the Father's joy. The weeping that has characterized many seasons of our lives is going to end, overwhelmed by the joy of the Lord. A new day begins to dawn for us as the dark shadows of those long nights are destroyed by the light of God's Word. God wants us to have the infectious power of a spiritual joy not predicated upon the situations of our lives but that wells up from deep inside our spirits.

Ahinoam

Like Abigail, this wife was also stolen by the Amalekites at Ziklag, but God helped David recover her safely and bring her to Hebron. Her name means "pleasantness," an important indicator of what God wants us to experience. He wants pleasantness to be restored in our lives. After going through traumatic and tragic experiences, it is easy to lose our pleasantness. Our ability to speak easily and lovingly with people and expect them to do the same with us is compromised. Hardship can make us seem bitter and our souls hardened and harsh. But in Hebron, God restores our pleasantness. We regain the calmness and peace that makes other people feel comforted in our presence, because we have been healed by the power of God.

Maacah

David also married the princess Maacah in Hebron. Her name means "pressed down" or "worn." She was a princess of the nation of Geshur, bordering Israel on the northeast corner. Because she was part of a royal family, David could not marry her until he was crowned king of Judah and in the right station to be her equal.

Maacah represents the complete restoration of what David was supposed to have as a wife in Saul's daughter Merab, who was taken from him and given to another man when David was in Gibeah. This was a political marriage, as was David's first marriage, to Michal, though they never were blessed to cement the union by having children together. But the successful marriage with Maacah created a strong bond for David between their two nations. She produced many children for David, essentially making up for Saul's broken promise of marriage to his daughter Merab. When you enter your Hebron, God is going to compensate you for relationships taken from you in the cities you had to escape from. He will be faithful in paying you back for what you had to leave behind to keep moving toward your promise. He is gracious enough to restore what you should have had.

Haggith

Another wife David took in Hebron was Haggith. In Hebrew, her name conveys the idea of festive dancing and celebration. When God brings you into your Hebron, He is going to usher in a season of celebration. He is going to make your heart dance. When the spirit of heaviness is finally removed from your life, you will be filled with praise, unbridled and uninhibited. When David brought the ark of the covenant into Jerusalem, he demonstrated some of this uninhibited dancing. This dancing did not start when he arrived in Jerusalem; it started while he was moving toward his goal. This is the lesson Haggith taught him and the lesson we must learn as well. We can't just dance in our

Jerusalem; we must learn to celebrate in Hebron first. If you can learn to celebrate being almost there, you can experience the joy of the journey.

What if we marked each place of advancement with a celebration? This type of mind-set would make each day so much lighter. In fact, David was dancing so joyously on the road to Jerusalem before he even arrived that he danced out of his clothes. This dancing made Michal rebuke David, but one can only imagine that Haggith was cheering him on. I can even see her joining him in the streets for the great celebration. Until we can dance in our Hebrons, we are not ready to dance in our Jerusalems. Part of the healing process is when God restores our ability to celebrate all along the way.

Abital

David's next wife named in the Scriptures was called Abital, which means "my Father is the dew." To understand what this name meant to David, it is important to study his writings. David used the word *tal*, or *dew*, only twice in all the Psalms. In both cases, it was used in the context of unity. In Psalm 110:3, he said that the people who are to be ruled "shall be willing in the day of thy power." He said they will operate in the beauty of holiness from the womb of the morning. And David closed this thought with the statement "Thou hast the dew of thy youth." The dew of youth falls when people are willing to work under God's appointed leadership. We see this theme again in 133:3, where he wrote that the unity of the brothers (association) was as if the dew that fell upon Mount Hermon would descend upon Jerusalem (Mount Zion). This is again a wonderful picture of what happens when unity is established in the life of a person. I believe that this unity is a strong part of the process of restoration in Hebron. In Ziklag, there was disunity, but in Hebron, Abital came into the life of David. God is the Father of dew. The garden of Eden was the paradise that God designed for man. The garden saw no rain, but God sent the dew to water the entire face of the earth (Gen. 2:6). No rain would fall until humanity was divided and man had completely rejected God's rulership. David's wife Abital is a sign that when we enter our Hebron, God is going to bring the kind of unity and peace to our relationships He intended for us when He created Eden. This unity will make the arid and sunbaked places in our lives as verdant and fertile as Mount Hermon.

Eglah

This is the last wife of Hebron mentioned by name in 1 Chronicles 3. She is, to me, one of the most important promises we can receive by studying the wives of Hebron. Her name means "calf," or "heifer." To understand the implication of her name, we have to look backward in the Torah to Joseph's interpretation of Pharaoh's dream, where the calves in the dream represented years. When God brought Eglah to David, she was a prophetic representation that God was returning years to his life.

According to scholars, Eglah bore David only one son while he was living in Hebron. His name was Ithream, which means "profit of the people," or "abundance." The years that God added to David's life would also give birth to abundance and profit for all the people. When we enter our Hebrons, God will return years to our lives as well. Sometimes we feel we have wasted so much time in the wrong cities, loitering too long in places that were not profitable. Imagine if God gave us back all the time we felt we'd lost. This alone would be a great reason to rejoice in our Hebrons. When we enter our Hebrons, God is going to add profitable years to our lives to make up for the ones we have lost.

Almost There

Volunteering with the children of the little bus ministry changed the course of my life. I began to study the Bible again, but this time I studied it so I could teach others. I learned the stories of the Old and New Testaments and discovered I had my mother's talent for bringing those stories to life. I also learned that I was very responsible. When assigned to look after children, I was relentlessly attentive to their safety. I fell in love with youth ministry, doing it simply for the joy of giving to others what I had missed. I loved being a mentor and teacher, watching children's eyes grow bright when the Scriptures became revelation that shone bright in the dark places of their lives. I loved encouraging children to dream big and reach far. I loved cheering them on like a father when they participated in competitions. I even looked forward to walking them safely back to their apartments after the programs ended. I learned the children's full names as well as the names of their parents or grandparents. I learned the kids' heights and shoe sizes. I discovered I had a sharp memory and could hold even the minutest detail in my memory, and I could read people's feelings just by looking them deep in their eyes. I learned that I was not a judgmental person and felt at home in almost any setting with people of every color and language.

I also discovered that I could lead. I could be trusted with another person's child and speak to anyone. I would walk right through drug deals and gangs to take someone's child to the door, and no one would bother me. I didn't see how I could do this full-time, because most of the pastors in my mother's church had to work secular jobs to support themselves and their families. I learned all of this about myself and knew I had found my calling. I couldn't imagine how it could become my life, but somehow I knew I was almost there.

12

JERUSALEM

The City of Dreams

As David prepared to move into Jerusalem, there was no way he could have known that the city he would first conquer and then establish would still stand three thousand years after his birth. There was no way he could have known his Jerusalem would be the epicenter for three of the world's major religions or that it would draw pilgrims from all over the world. There was no way David could have known the city of his dreams would have so much value to billions of people or that it would have so much value to a boy from Boston, a city on a continent David did not even know existed.

Jerusalem was a dream of David's heart, a promise that twinkled in the eye of this valiant Hebrew soldier. Jerusalem was to be the culmination of his quest—the city he could put his own name on and where he would establish a temple to worship the God he loved. It was the place he carried in his heart as he traveled through each city. It was the end of his quest for the crown but just the beginning of his life as a king. David would live there until he was seventy years old. He would dance in the streets in joy, weep over the loss of his children, and finally be laid to rest there. And upon his tomb, the faithful would build a synagogue and offer prayers to Jehovah some three thousand years later. This was the miracle of his dreams: that his Jerusalem would so far outlive him even when other great cities of that time would pass away.

Today one of the greatest pleasures of my life is taking people to the holy city of Jerusalem. Twice a year, depending on my speaking schedule, I am blessed to lead Holy Land tours. I love taking people there and watching the Bible come alive to them as we traverse the sands of time and walk in the footsteps of Abraham, David, and Jesus. I love singing praise songs in the Hebrew language and reciting the psalms in the very land where they were written. And I love watching people's hearts open and their eyes weep as they walk into the lands they have heard about for their entire lives of faith. All of the Holy Land contains a unique charm. As the shroud of history is slowly removed and the context of the surroundings demonstrates the accuracy of Scripture, people are dumbfounded by the historicity of our sacred writings. The context allows the Bible to be more than a stolid book of cold characters; it becomes a thriving canvas for the imagination to further paint in the details. It makes the text we preach become vivid and vibrant.

I have taken pastors, business leaders, college students, house-wives, and retirees. No matter who they are, they are inevitably changed by the experience. Each night I hold court in a little café and we drink strong Arabic coffee mixed with cardamom and sit up until the early dawn breaks across the horizon, welcomed by

the song of the muezzin. We talk about not only what we saw
and learned on the day's journey but also how it made us feel.
To me, the spiritual impact of our walks through the Holy Land
have greater value than the historical instruction. Some things
can be taught to us, but others can only be caught by us. They
are absorbed and understood at the level of the spirit. I am so
honored to facilitate this process in the lives of people in which,
within the context of Jerusalem, the content comes to life and we
feel the power of God. I have been so privileged that my ministry
has carried me around the world, but still I have discovered no
city as dear to my heart or as influencial to my spirit as the city
of Jerusalem.

Anyone who talks to me for more than five minutes quickly
discovers I still have a deep fondness for the city of my birth; the
water of Boston Harbor still flows in my veins. I am without question a New Englander, and each summer my soul is summoned
to the brown sands of Martha's Vineyard. But even my beloved
Boston does not compare with Jerusalem.

My wife and I lived in Dallas for almost twenty years. I fell
in love with the spicy food, the hot weather, and the bighearted
people. It was in Dallas that I found my mentor and pastor, Bishop
T. D. Jakes, and where I found my voice in ministry. I really began
to believe that, with God's providence, I could have an impact on
the youth of my generation. But not even Dallas is as dear to me
as the city of Jerusalem.

Jerusalem represents the place we have been on a quest to
reach. It is not our final destination, just the city where we begin
to live out our God-given purpose. In the other cities, we were

equipped and fully furnished as individuals to complete our true assignments. Many of us will never realize just how many people will benefit from the cities we build. They have impact far beyond our lifetimes, and many will feel the positive results from the sacrifices we have made to reach our Jerusalems. Our dreams for our lives are finite, but God's dreams lived out through our lives are always eternal.

THE FINAL PIECES

Before we fully walk with David into his Jerusalem, we must deal with the final puzzle pieces of his process that preceded his promotion. He had a few more things that had to fall into place that serve as indicators for him, and us, of when it would be time to leave Hebron and enter Jerusalem. This is important and instructive to us because when we examine David's walk, we are given clues to what God is preparing to do in our lives.

When we see (1) the introduction of an imitation, (2) the division of the enemy, (3) the death of shame, (4) the agreement of the elders, and (5) the conquering of the strongholds of the past, we know it's time to walk into our Jerusalems.

Introduction of an Imitation

Word came to David while he was still in Ziklag that Saul had died. One might think the elimination of his primary enemy would signal David's swift rise as ruler of Israel, "but Abner the son of Ner, commander of Saul's army, took Ishbosheth the son of

Saul and brought him over to Mahanaim; and he made him king over … all Israel" (2 Sam. 2:8–9 NKJV).

Sometimes the battle seems so long and the journey so difficult that when we hear that the primary obstacle has been removed, we become so overjoyed that we do not steel our hearts for more struggle. Beware of premature celebrating, because sometimes there is still hard news to come. In David's case, the next thing he heard after the news of Saul's death was that Abner, the Benjamite general, took the last surviving son of King Saul, Ishbosheth, and crowned him king. Abner was a powerful general and an influential leader. So instead of the battle being over, it had simply fallen into the hands of a new leader. The intent to destroy David and conquer his troops was still present. The baton had been passed to Saul's son. Ishbosheth was crowned king of all the tribes of Israel except Judah, and David had not yet walked fully into the prophecy and purpose Samuel had told him about way back in Bethlehem.

Certainly David had to have been disappointed, but he was not deterred, because the impostor must always precede the intended. In fact, the rise of the *imitation* is a sign that the *authentic* is on the way. We see this picture played out over and over throughout Scripture. Ishmael came before Isaac. Esau came before Jacob. Reuben came before Joseph. The order in which we are introduced has no bearing on the outcome, because the order is to the divine destiny God has prepared for our lives.

Jesus outlined this principle when He said, "The last shall be first, and the first last" (Matt. 20:16). This demonstrates that seniority might impact what people see, but it does not carry the same weight with God. This is critical to our thinking if we are to handle the emotional turmoil that comes when an imitation is promoted over us.

We have to pass the season of testing before we can be trusted. Many people short-circuit their own promotion because they do not respond well to the delay when they thought they had arrived. Joshua had to be a spy for Moses before he could lead Israel. Elisha had to pour water on the hands of the man who carried the mantle before he could catch it. This is how God usually works in our lives: He tests us to see if we can be faithful over a few things before He makes us ruler over much (25:23).

Saul had one of the fastest elevations in all of Scripture. His rise was so meteoric that it surprised even him. He was not given a period of testing or granted a time of preparation before he was thrust into ruling, and the immaturity and insecurity he brought to the throne were evident. David was processed in each city even as he progressed through them. Your progression is the process of your promotion, so never lose hope. When God gives you a promise and then reveals your purpose, you can count on it. But our hearts should be grateful for the process, because it is making us ready to retain the blessing He will pour into our lives.

Imitations are needed to help people better discern the authentic. God will allow the imitation to arise first so people can truly determine your authenticity. Do not allow that period of imitation to discourage you. Let the imitator's rise encourage you, because it is just one of the puzzle pieces that must fall into place before you can enter your Jerusalem.

Division of the Enemy

The next indicator that God is positioning you to enter your Jerusalem is when you begin to see division arise in the camp of your adversary. In the case of David, a division arose between Abner and Ishbosheth. But the Bible says they did not fall out over the war effort. They did not argue over Abner's failed attempts to quell the insurrection of the tribe of Judah or over how to run the rest of his kingdom; these two men fell out over a woman. The young king, Ishbosheth, accused Abner of having sex with one of his father's concubines. At that time, taking a concubine of a king was a way of staking a claim to the throne. Scripture is not clear on whether this tryst actually happened. What we do know is that Ishbosheth believed that the rumors were true. When he boldly brought the allegations to his general, the two parted company in anger.

The Old Testament has many stories of battles when the Lord caused the enemies of the children of Israel to turn on themselves. God is not the author of confusion, but He will allow contention in the ranks of your adversaries, causing them to fight among themselves. This will clear the path for you to step into your destiny. You can simply stand confidently as the division destroys your enemy. Do not allow yourself to be baited into skirmishes or petty wars that toxic people have with each other. Do not allow them to pull you in. Just keep doing what God has called you to do and trust Him to work out the details.

As Ishbosheth and Abner were dividing their country, David just kept on ruling in Hebron, giving leadership to the people of Judah and waiting patiently for God to handle it. God always shapes our environments before He allows us to fill them. He created the oceans first and the fish after. He created the heavens and then the birds. He created the garden of Eden before placing Adam and Eve there. As you are waiting for your Jerusalem, trust that God is creating the atmosphere that will sustain you, that He is preparing something great: the city of your dreams. He is removing the obstacles and hindrances that would cause you trouble in your future. It is not always easy to wait, particularly when you have waited so long. But the greater the wait, the greater the reward.

Probably unbeknownst to you right now, God is allowing your enemy to be divided and cleared out of the way. Then you can walk into your Jerusalem without worrying about being attacked, hassled, or hurt by that adversary ever again.

Death of Shame

This next indicator is perhaps the most telling. As I studied the Scriptures to unearth this key, I found so much personal healing. I learned the Hebrew meaning of the name Ishbosheth, and it gave me such encouragement that I had to pause to give God praise for the level of understanding and release that came from the discovery. Ishbosheth in Hebrew means "the man of shame." Why would anyone name their son a man of shame? Why would anyone want to hang that label around the neck of an innocent child? It is particularly surprising when you consider that Saul named his oldest son Jonathan, which means "gift of God." I believe that the name was providentially placed for our benefit—put there for our instruction and encouragement—because David could not become the king of his Jerusalem until the man of shame died.

Often it is our own shame that limits us from entering our Jerusalem. We are still so caught up in our pasts that the blessings God has for our futures are out of reach. This can cause us so much pain because we are ready in many other ways for the advancement and placement we have been promised, but we are still prisoners of our own shame. We are imprisoned by our pride, because we have not fully accepted the grace God freely offers for our lives.

I have stood around the altar with people still wrestling with the shame of things from long ago. They prayed and cried for deliverance but still could not release the shame. God has already offered to fully heal those wounds, yet I have prayed with countless people who could not believe that God still loved them. Shame is one of the greatest hindrances to our deliverance and subsequently a mighty anchor that keeps us from flying. The way we felt after we went through the traumas can blind us from the reality that we are still alive, that we have indeed survived, and that God has given us the amazing grace to walk boldly into the next city.

As I began to minister to people, I kept my childhood experiences secret. I thought the shame of being a foster child, living in the streets, and being abandoned by my father would cause those I sought to reach to look down on me. I acted as if I had not gone through hell, yet the people who continued to listen to me and follow my ministry could clearly detect that I understood their pain. Out of shame, I stayed silent for so many years. I knew that the Bible teaches us we are overcome by the blood of the Lamb and the word of our testimony (Rev. 12:11), but I could not tell them the story of how my own life had been changed by that blood; the shame I had allowed to attach to my own life had not yet been fully expunged. I understood it intellectually, but I did not want to be viewed as a victim, so I hid the truth of the miracles of my life. I was afraid people would view me as damaged goods. I did not know that the reason people kept inviting me to speak and filling up my events was because they could sense I was a broken person being repaired by the blood of the Lamb. They were attracted because they were also broken in places and needed that same blood to bring them healing. I was dutiful in pointing them to God's grace, but I had neglected the powerful truth that my testimony could help others find their own spiritual healing.

I rose from being an assistant youth pastor to becoming a youth pastor in my own right. I was hosting weekly events attracting thousands of young people, preaching in churches, and appearing on a worldwide television broadcast, but I kept the story of my own life under close wraps. It wasn't even that I was ashamed of the things I had done; I was ashamed of the things I had survived. In some ways I kept it quiet so as not to bring embarrassment to my family; at least that's what I told myself. I also held these secrets for years because I was ashamed of where I had come from and I did not want to be another statistic or sad story. But the more I shook the shackles of shame off my mind and heart and was bold enough to open my mouth to share my story, the more I realized I was not so different from other people.

I tried to fit in with those who had been raised in two-parent homes, thinking that they were better than me because they had grown up in safe and comfortable environments. It was not until

I began to sit with people in counseling sessions that I learned that pain is not prejudiced; it visits every home and plagues every family. By listening to people, I learned that it was possible for a child to still feel abandoned and alone in a two-parent home. Parents who are physically present but emotionally unavailable are just as damaging as parents who are physically unavailable. I learned that the ideal white-picket-fence life could not defend against the pains that visit the impoverished ghettos of the inner city. We all are advancing toward our own Jerusalems. None of us is born in the city of his or her dreams. We are born in a Bethlehem—in a nondescript and unsung city—where God sends our prophetic assignments. We can experience our tomorrows only if we walk out of our yesterdays, but shame has the power to keep us locked in the past. In the process of handing out the medicine of grace, I was allowed to partake of the same medicine, and my shame began to fade.

Our secret shame separates us, but if we could dare to be open with one another, we would discover that despite our racial, socioeconomic, or religious differences, we all have faced similar pain. The names and faces are different, but the struggle is the same. Ishbosheth has to die so we can be free. As long as that shame reigns in our lives, we cannot enter our Jerusalems. The Bible tells us Ishbosheth was assassinated while he lay in his bed. It is vital that we not allow shame to sleep in our castle. As long as shame lives there, we cannot take up residence in the future we are supposed to have. The removal of the impostor king paved the way for Israel to finally embrace Samuel's prophecy and allow David to fulfill the covenant, anointing him king. Until we shed our shame, we cannot fully be what God intends for us to become.

What realms are awaiting you? What doors are invisible to you because the shadow of shame has blocked your eyes? Freeing yourself from even the appetite for shame is a clear indicator that God is getting you ready to walk into your Jerusalem.

Agreement of the Elders

While David was in Hebron, all the elders of the entire nation of Israel, not just the elders of Judah, came to him and made a covenant. Together they anointed him to be their king. David, who had been warring with the other tribes for years, was finally embraced by the elders. The questions he had about his divine purpose were answered, and the realm of service he had longed to fulfill was open to him. He was not yet in his Jerusalem. He was not in a position to establish his throne in Zion. He had not even conquered the citadel of Jebus, which he would rename Jerusalem. But this was the indicator that his long-held dream was not an illusion or the machinations of his own ambition. The elders, the leaders of his nation, came to add their collective agreement to what he had known to be true of himself for so long.

Faith causes us to dream seemingly outlandish dreams at times, and we might question their legitimacy. Sometimes we may question our sanity. You are just about to enter into your Jerusalem when God sends elders—people of experience and respect—to confirm your dream. You might have had to nurture that dream single-handedly for many years, but at this next stage, there is grace from God on your life and you are on the right path. The elders will take of their oil—their prayers and their spiritual understanding—and mark you so all who doubted will have to agree with what God has done. The agreement of the elders is critical because they will bring their gravitas, conviction, and reputations to your calling. David was assigned by God and by men to be shepherd of His people and to be ruler over Israel (2 Sam. 5:2).

When God sets you up to "rule," He means that you are to be the shepherd. Do not confuse these concepts, because only God is the true king. Whatever gift, talent, responsibility, or realm God has given you, He never gives you ownership of that gift; He simply invests you with the responsibility to shepherd it. Jerusalem is too big to take on alone. You will need the agreement of elders to fully execute the purpose of God.

I will never forget the day I was ordained. I had been serving as the youth pastor of my home church in Boston. The group had grown from sixty-five teenagers to well over a thousand. I was speaking throughout the region and had even been asked to travel around the country to teach and instruct other youth pastors on how to develop an urban ministry. I networked with leaders from around the country, speaking to them with an inspiring message of hope that had been birthed out of my own pain and struggle, but I had not yet been ordained. In our churches, ordination did not precede position. Most often we were assigned to work in a position and if we demonstrated grace from God to operate in that area, the elders would come alongside to confirm that role with the gift of ordination.

I remember the day clearly, because it was the outward confirmation of what I had been doing for so long. Those early bus-ministry days had prepared my heart to lead young people to Christ. The training I had garnered through volunteering in secular student-led organizations had prepared me to lead teams of young adults in the building of regionwide outreaches and events. I did not feel fully ready to lead, but the elders of our church agreed it was time for me to receive that role, surrounded by their prayers and blessings.

On the evening of Sunday, May 5, 1996, the Right Reverend Dr. Joseph Garlington led a small presbytery of pastors who anointed me with oil and officially set me aside for Christian ministry. I had never had a father to affirm me in my calling, but on that day, Dr. Garlington stepped into that paternal role for me and became one of my spiritual fathers. He birthed me in the Spirit as minister of the gospel. My pastor at the time, the Right Reverend Dr. Gideon Thompson, prayed powerfully over me and officially installed me as the youth pastor of our church. My wife stood beside me as we took up together the call to reach the next generation.

I fully knew and understood this to be my divine purpose. I had already started doing the work God called me to, but that day had significance to me because I had such respect for these men of God, and their affirmation only served to give me greater confidence that the dreams I'd had since I was a little boy were not just my imagination; they were becoming true in my life. I had received many promises about my future. The sainted people of my little church had told me in detail what God wanted to do in my life. They were the Samuels God used to anoint me in my Bethlehem. But this was not the small church I was raised in; this was the largest church in our region, and these were men of God

used by the Lord to influence people far and wide. Dr. Thompson
was learned and astute, and Dr. Garlington had ministered the
message of racial and spiritual reconciliation to people all around
the world.

My mother was not there and neither was my father, but I felt
the overwhelming embrace of my heavenly Father so strongly I
could barely stand under the emotion of that moment. I was not
the only person ordained that day, but to me there was no one else
in the room. The elders surrounded me, and as they prayed, all I
had suffered in my past began to make sense. I knew without question or any equivocation that I was on my way to my Jerusalem. I
was so close, because the elders had finally arrived.

The church I now shepherd does not belong to me; every
soul God has trusted me to look after belongs to Him. God has
entrusted me in this season of life with the awesome task of shep-
herding what belongs to Him. The Lord also has given my wife
and me two wonderful sons, but I do not rule over them; it is my
job to work with my wife to prayerfully lead them and guide them
into their God-given purpose. This is the case with every "king."
We can rule only what we are willing to care for. When the elders
come to anoint you, you will know that your Jerusalem is just
moments away. The dream is now coming to pass, and God has
prepared you to walk into the city of your dreams.

Conquering the Strongholds of the Past

David was crowned king of all Israel after reigning over Judah
for seven and a half years. He passed the test of promotion in his

Hebron and received the covenant endorsement of all the elders of Israel. But his battles were not over. His struggles were not at an end. In many respects, his real battles were just beginning. His Hebron was not his Jerusalem. Hebron was just the gateway to battle—the entrance to his greatest victories. This is also true in your life. Your anointing is never the end of your journey; it is only the beginning, and no anointing is ever solely for your benefit. God anoints you to do something that will help other people's lives as well. He is too economical to make your Jerusalem about you alone. The establishment of Jerusalem is for the benefit of many people.

In Jerusalem, David built a tabernacle of worship that would bless his entire nation. And later in Jerusalem, David's son Solomon would erect a majestic temple to the Lord that would become the center of worship of Jehovah in Israel for well over four hundred years. Jerusalem would bless the nations and become the place where the Savior of the world would face trial, judgment, and crucifixion and then be resurrected. Jerusalem was much bigger than David; it outlived him by thousands of years. Even when conquered and seemingly destroyed over and over, it rose from the ashes and became, as it is today, a beacon of hope to all who put their trust in the Lord.

Jerusalem was not handed to David on a silver platter. The Jebusites who had been occupying that land did not concede the territory to David just because the Israelites had crowned him king. The Jebusites had occupied that stronghold since before the time of Joshua and had no intention of giving it up easily. The were defiant because they believed their city could not be breached. They had food and water enough to outlast any siege. Their city was naturally fortified because of its elevated position and reinforced by the strongest walls in Canaan. They believed that their weakest warriors could defend these walls, and they rained down taunts upon the heads of David and his troops from their lofty positions of presumed safety. But they didn't know David. He was not one to look for an easy way out. He had fought through too much and for far too long to be discouraged by mere man-made walls.

When you have had to walk through hell and high water and through the intimidation of your giants, the attempts of little people to intimidate you are always fruitless if you remember what God has brought you through. The hardship of your journey only crystallizes your resolve and makes you ready to do whatever is both godly and necessary to reach your divine purpose. The Jebusites had dug in, but David was grounded in the truth of who he was and what God had purposed for his life. People like David are unstoppable. It is not that they are perfect, but these people fight to win. They risk even their own indignity and withstand all kinds of verbal abuse, ignoring the words of naysayers and false prophets. They have learned to ignore the statistics and negative reports because they have a faith that is stronger than their circumstances and a belief that belies their situation. They have too much skin in the game to back up now and know too much about their God to run away scared.

High walls did not intimidate Joshua, though the walls were able to stop him. But David was not even intimidated by the barriers that thwarted his forefathers. He had been living in a divine promise too long to doubt God. When you are free from the memory of what defeated your predecessors, you are truly free. Just because an obstacle stopped someone else in your family or even in your past generations, that does not mean it can stop you. Faith married to divine purpose is too powerful to be intimidated by any wall. We must learn this faith focus from David: we must not be intimidated by the shadows of the past, because God wants us to walk in the bright light of our present-day faith.

I could have allowed my father's negligence as a husband and parent to discourage me from marrying and believing I could be a successful father, but I mustered the faith to believe that the mountain of generational fatherlessness could be removed from my life and my family. The promise of my destiny was stronger than the mountain of my past. I just had to believe that it was so.

Believing is not easy when you have had no models of success. But David did not allow the lack of success of his predecessors to deter him from his destiny. When you put feet to your faith, the walls come down and the obstacles are removed, no matter how long those walls have withstood others. Until you learn how to ignore circumstances, you will be paralyzed with fear. When faith in your divine purpose is exercised with relentless action, no walls can stop you from reaching your divinely purposed goals. God is able to give you both the faith and the victory; He requires only that you put that faith into action. When you do that, the impossible becomes possible.

UP THE GUTTERS

David had a plan. He had been carefully studying the defenses of this citadel for as long as he could remember. His hometown of Bethlehem was only six miles away from Jebus, so it is entirely possible he had been in and around this city since he was a little boy. Perhaps he brought the young lambs of Bethlehem or the barley harvest from his father's fields to be sold at market. In the course of his travels here, he noticed a weakness—a small chink in the armor of their defenses that could be exploited by an army the size of the unified forces of Israel that were now completely at his disposal. He did not attempt this attack when he was the captain of his wayward band of soldiers. But once he had unity in his nation and was in charge of all the troops, his first military action (that we are told of) was to take the city that had defied them since the time Joshua led the invasion of the land. David devised a plan involving an overlooked part of the fortress. He targeted the gutters of the city as a way to breach its walls. He told his men to scale those gutters through the debris and the waste of the city to access the battle towers. He offered the rank of captain to anyone who completed the climb (2 Sam. 5:8). He challenged the men to have no regard for how they would look, smell, or feel in order to get this victory. He instructed them to attack the place no one else would consider, because sometimes victory requires the willingness to do what no one else will.

We often are defeated because we want to win and still be pristine, but battle is both bloody and dirty. The battlefields of 1000 BC were not tidy places. The smell of blood and feces rose from the field of battle as dead men's bodies loosed their bowels. The screams of ravens and the tearing of flesh by scavengers were the only sounds that rose above the hopeless moans of wounded and dying men. David was no stranger to the horrors of the battlefield, and he knew that his troops had to be prepared for the same eventuality. This is why he asked them to wade through the waste of the city and climb up the unguarded roof to find victory on the other side of the wall.

Hidden in Trouble

God uses waste to camouflage us from the attack of the Enemy. We see this theme repeated throughout the Bible. Moses was saved from infanticide by being hidden away in a basket covered with pitch and slime. This ugly basket was set afloat from the banks of the Nile River, carrying him past the hippos and crocodiles into the arms of a princess. The ark of Moses was ugly but effective (Exod. 2). We see this in the ministry of Jonah when he was vomited out of the belly of the great fish to reach the ears of the Ninevites (Jon. 2:10–3:10). We also see this in the life of Joseph. God used slavery to place him in Egypt, knowing that from the pit, he would be elevated to a position of higher power (Gen. 37). The cross seemed so final and the situation so ugly that the Devil had no idea God would use the camouflage of Calvary to position Jesus to conquer him for all time. But the putrid smell of death was simply covering the greatest victory that ever would be won—one that would plunder hell and the grave for all eternity and set men free. All the pain of my childhood—the abandonment, hunger, loneliness, and despair—was just the cover God used to position me into the purpose He had willed for me from the beginning of my life and the beginning of time.

Many times God will challenge you to get dirty, stinky, and slimy in order to fulfill His divine purpose for your life. The ugly things are merely camouflage so God can move you into the right position without the Enemy detecting your movement. The Devil won't see you coming, because your circumstances are so ugly that he believes that you are down for the count. The Enemy is so busy having a party over how bad your situation looks that he never considers that God is using the ugly situation, the inglorious position, to place you for power. Your present trouble is not always a hindrance; it often is a means to a greater end.

THANK-YOU LETTER

The men of Jebus had such confidence in their defenses that they declared boldly that even the lame and the blind could defend their walls by simply hurling stones, arrows, or hot oil down on the heads of anyone who tried to breach their thick walls. But they had not counted on anyone using the cover of the gutters to shield them from stones. They had never encountered a general willing to get that dirty.

When you have climbed through the gutters of life, despair, and loneliness, man-made gutters have no hold on you. Some of the most pained people become the most powerful. God turns pain into power to fulfill His divine purpose, and this can be the story for all of us. Defeat is temporary for those willing to fight until they win. The welfare mother willing to take government assistance and withstand the indignity of judgmental stares can finish her education and get a job that will pull her family out of the pit of poverty. The lowest-level office worker can become company president by remaining undaunted by an inauspicious start and being determined to stick it out. Destiny sometimes calls us to get dirty, but we can always wash the dirt off when we win. Contrarily, the stains of defeat are permanent for those unwilling to do whatever is godly and necessary to reach their goals. God resists the proud and gives greater grace to the humble (James 4:6). David was humble enough to get dirty, and God was gracious enough to give victory.

David should have written the Jebusites a thank-you letter for building the gutters that provided the only way into their city. He should have congratulated them for making the cover that would allow his soldiers to take their city. Had there been no gutters, there would have been no victory. Had there been no closed-in, smelly places, David and his men would have had no means of entry.

It would be a great exercise for us to write thank-you letters to the people, situations, and past problems that provided the cover for us to climb into our Jerusalems. I have led many people in this activity over the years so they could understand that what was intended to destroy them only made them stronger. They were made wiser and better as a result of the climb, and the Devil never knew what hit him once they got into their rightful position. The gutters are something I praise God for now. I thank Him for the loneliness because it taught me to appreciate my real friends. I thank Him for the fatherlessness because it taught me to appreciate my mentors and surrogate fathers. I thank Him for the days of hunger because it taught me to be compassionate to those in need. I even thank God for the years I spent in foster care because they taught me how to foster other people into their God-given purpose. I thank Him for the rejection because it taught me how to accept people of every color, country, and creed. I have written so many thank-you letters, even to my own father because his absence taught me how to rely on God as my heavenly Father.

I have shared these truths around the world. These are hard-won truths, truths I had to fight for, truths I had to cry for, but truths that set me free. I am honored to be allowed to share these truths with you, as I believe that they have the power to set you free and push you one step closer to your Jerusalem.

CHANGE THE NAME

When you refer to the situations of your life as ugly, it frames the way you view them, but when you can start calling them beautiful, it begins to change your perspective. This is the way you discover you are more than a conqueror (Rom. 8:37). David renamed Jebus Jerusalem, which means "city of peace." It seems preposterous that he would pick this name for the place he won through a long and hard-fought war. But changing your narrative—what you say about your life—is an important step for walking into your Jerusalem. Stop naming things after what you have already conquered and start calling them by the things you have been promised. God is going to give you a place of peace, even if you have to battle for it, so don't let the battle define how you see it. Celebrate the fact that you survived. Say thank you and rename the situation. The Bible says, "Death and life are in the power of the tongue" (Prov. 18:21). Start renaming and rewriting your life story. By changing the narrative, you will change your perspective and find peace. Making peace with your past struggles frees you to enjoy the future God always intended for you to enjoy.

Call the hard beginnings your Bethlehem. Call the places of betrayal Keilah. Call the places where you felt surrounded by enemies Ziklag. By renaming them, you will be reminded that you are still walking toward your goal. You are in motion, not stuck in place. Your story is still being written and rewritten by both you and the Lord. He is cowriting your narrative by faith. You are walking to your Jerusalem.

Move into Your Purpose

David dwelled in the fort and called it the city of David. And he went on and grew great, and the Lord was with him (2 Sam. 5:9–10). Once you reach your Jerusalem, you may have to initially force yourself to move in. Relax in it and revel in it. You really do deserve to enjoy the things God has promised you. I have met people who finally made it into their dream job, dream house, or even their dream relationship, but because they were scarred from their past battles, they could not enjoy the fruits of their victory. They lived each day on pins and needles, just waiting for the bottom to fall out. They stood on the outside of their victory and never settled into it. You may have grown so used to warfare that you never allow yourself to enjoy peacetime. Armor is not made to be worn permanently and weapons are not to be carried while living in the house.

In the spring of 2010, I became the senior pastor of The Potter's House of Denver. I had traveled as an evangelist, speaking in churches and conferences for about seven years prior. I had grown used to living out of suitcases and running from planes to podiums. Sleeping in hotels had caused me to be a light sleeper, and living with the adrenaline that comes from speaking as many as eight times a day had caused me to be so on edge I could hardly relax.

After years of praying that God would send me to a city and give me a church to serve, one would think I could finally relax. I anticipated that arriving at this long-awaited Jerusalem in my life, I would heave a sigh of relief and rest in the blessing. But it took me a long time to exhale and relax. For almost two years, I continued to battle within myself. I was waiting for the proverbial other shoe to drop and for someone to come out of the shadows and take it all away. I didn't sell our house in Dallas and refused to let myself believe Denver was where God would allow me to rest. Then one day it dawned on me what I was doing, so I got into my truck and drove around the city and began introducing myself over and over again. I started to call Denver "My Denver." I started to call the pulpit of the church "My See." I started to call the Front Range of the Rocky Mountains "My Mountains." I called the cold and crystal-clear lakes "My Lakes."

I started looking for a neighborhood to live in permanently. I began to meet the city officials and introduce myself to the other pastors in the region. I still travel and speak from time to time, but I have moved my heart into Denver and allowed my peace to settle here. I introduced myself to the local barista, made friends with the dry cleaner, met my next-door neighbors, and walked my dogs around our new neighborhood so they would know we are home. I learned from David: Bethlehem was where he was born, but Jerusalem was where he decided to dwell.

BUILD IT UP

David did not just move into the citadel and leave it as he found it; no, he instantly began to make changes. Moving in is just the first stage. You have to build up your city. This sweat equity is what solidifies your connection to where you are. David worked from the outside in. He started with the ramparts in Millo and worked his way into the city, reinforcing its walls and then establishing his own house. No Jerusalem comes to you ready-made, and the process of remaking it ensures it is truly yours.

After my first two years in Denver, I started leading the church in beautification processes. We laid down grass and planted more trees. We excavated the gravel in the parking lot and laid concrete. We hung new signs and installed new lights. This seemed like cosmetic work to some, but to me it was the culmination of what I had been dreaming. Like an expectant mother who prepares the nursery, I started to prepare the church for the arrival of new people. When the crew came out to pour the concrete, I could barely contain myself. I knew that the process of improving our church meant I was becoming more connected with my destiny. You have to say, "Jerusalem, I am so glad I am finally here. But in order for me to feel settled, I'll need to remake you into the image of my own dreams." When God gives you a divine purpose, He does not give you all the details; He leaves the details to your own design. Just as with Adam, God made all the animals but left it to Adam to name them (Gen. 2:19–20). God could have named them, but He wanted Adam to have a sense of ownership and a sense of home.

When you reach your Jerusalem, decide to not only move in but also build it up. This is the truest sign that you are home—that you have arrived for the good of the city.

GROW GREATER

As you build up your new city of destiny, you must also continue building up yourself. Jerusalem is not the place to stop growing as a person. Attaining your dream and stepping into your calling doesn't mean you stop pressing on. Growth is part of life, and therefore growth should be the goal of every person. David grew in his Jerusalem and so must you. You have to determine within yourself that you will not become complacent in your Jerusalem, for this a trap that limits so many.

Once you have discovered your God-given purpose and are allowed to move into it, you have to decide to grow greater as a person. Develop the new skill sets this city requires. Cultivate the resources needed for operating in this new arena. Read the new manuals, attend the pertinent workshops, and revamp your own paradigms to maximize your time in this new city. Jerusalem is not a place of stagnation but a place of growth. Even though it might take you more than twenty years to reach the goal, as it did with King David, Jerusalem represents a new beginning, not an ending.

I think of how my mother would buy clothes for us at the beginning of the school year. Because we struggled financially, she would buy my clothes a size too big. In her wisdom, she knew that those school clothes had to last the entire school year, and by getting them bigger, I could grow into them. This is what God does with us. He puts us into a larger arena so we will be challenged to grow into it. He wants us to grow greater emotionally and spiritually as human beings, businesspeople, church leaders, parents, and spouses. It is a compliment to our heavenly Father when we fully develop our divine purpose and start to grow in grace and knowledge of who He really is in our lives.

He Is Still with You

Even though you have reached your Jerusalem, God does not withdraw from you. Jerusalem is not the place to abandon Him. You will need Him as much in your Jerusalem as you needed Him in all the other cities. Your spiritual relationship is not put on hold just because you have arrived. In reality, it has to kick into a higher gear, because you are now doing things on a scale you have never seen before. Jerusalem is the place where your relationship with God has to deepen so you will be prepared to win the new battles you face.

The "Lord of hosts" is a military term. David had to receive revelation that God was the Lord of his battles, as he would fight some of his greatest battles in and from Jerusalem, including with the Philistines and other enemies of Israel. He also would fight his own temptation regarding his affair with Bathsheba and the rebellion of his own sons, first Amnon and later Absalom. David would need to discover and rediscover that the Lord was with him.

In heaven, there will be no struggles. In heaven, there will be no hard decisions to make. In heaven, you will not do battle. But Jerusalem is not heaven, and your divine purpose needs to be fulfilled on earth. As long as you are here, your comfort is knowing that the God of the universe is fighting with you and for you. He is the Lord of hosts, always standing with you, even in your Jerusalem.

CONCLUSION

The path David followed to achieve his God-given purpose covered a large portion of his life. What started in Bethlehem with his anointing came to fruition with his crowning in Jerusalem. Although connected, these highlights were separated by a number of key events in his life that were essential for molding him and preparing him for the leader he would become. As we walked with David through his journey, we visited the many cities that shaped his life and his future.

We all take a similar journey, though for some it may be a shorter process than David's, and for others it may take an entire lifetime. By learning from David's experience, it is possible to identify what city we are in and what God is trying to show us there. The length of time we stay in any city is determined by how attuned we are to what God is teaching us and how He is shaping us for our callings.

In Bethlehem, the city of beginnings, we found David as a shepherd boy, clueless about the enormity of what lay ahead. But his seemingly insignificant origin was not an indication of where he would end up. The same is true in our lives. Regardless of how we start out, God has a great plan for where we will go and what He can accomplish through us.

In Gibeah, the city of exposure, David was exposed to Saul's court, learning what makes a good leader. He was able to avoid many of the mistakes Saul made by being in a position to observe. This stage might not feel important for advancing our positions, but it is essential for developing and preparing us for where we are headed.

In the valley of Elah, the city of transition, David took a great leap forward in his journey when he battled Goliath. He went from being unknown to widely celebrated in one swift motion. These key moments are powerful for our lives and our advancement, but we can miss them if we are not listening to God and following His leading.

Jebus, the city of personal promise, is where David laid down the marker, establishing a covenant with his own future. We also must be deliberate in the goals we set for ourselves as we commit to our futures in order to maintain the momentum gained from our transition cities and fuel us toward the next.

David's second stop in Gibeah was a time of re-equipping. It is easy to feel in this city that we are losing ground. But remember that retreat does not necessarily mean surrender. It is important, particularly after such dramatic advancement, to take the time to reassess where we are and learn the skills and gather the tools necessary for what lies ahead.

Gath was also an important place in that it was where David found a moment to catch his breath, even though he was sitting in enemy territory. He was shielded from the relentless pursuit of Saul, and that gave him an opportunity to regroup and prepare for the next step forward. Even though David did not seek God's guidance in making this move, it teaches us a valuable lesson about God's willingness to use our mistakes to work toward our good and keep us moving toward His purpose for our lives.

Adullum was essential to David's preparation for stepping into his greater role as leader of a nation. So often God tests our ability to handle the full measure of our purposes by giving us smaller responsibilities as a trial run. We should regard every opportunity as a chance to learn and grow, never dismissing any request as beneath us.

In Keilah, En Gedi, and Ziklag, David faced some of the most difficult challenges of his life. He endured betrayal, disappointment, discouragement, and temptation. He faced some of the most important trials for shaping him as a leader. As we move toward our Jerusalems, we will come into cities like these, perhaps causing us to feel hopeless and defeated. But we should not allow these stages to distract us from where God is taking us, because they all prepare us for the fullness of His purpose for our lives.

Hebron is the city of "almost there," and it can be tempting to see this as the final destination. It can be easy to think we are ready and have arrived. We should not stop here, as it is not our ultimate place of purpose. This city reminds us to celebrate each step of the journey and keep our eyes on God to know where He really wants us.

Jerusalem is where we finally possess the promise—the destiny—God has planned for us from the beginning. But the greatest lesson we can learn in this city is that it is not our last stop. It really is the starting point for the greatest part of our journey, because it is here that we move into the life God has been preparing us to live and the work He intends for us to do.

Throughout this journey, I have shared my own story of finding my way to the calling I felt on my life as a small boy. I revealed the struggle and heartache I endured as I faced many periods of feeling alone and lost. Those experiences could have turned me into a bitter and hopeless man. Thankfully, I had the foundation of my faith in God, because those trials taught me how to relate to the many types of hurting people I would encounter in my ministry.

I found my Jerusalem in Denver when I allowed myself to settle into how God wanted to use me there. But I know my journey is far from over. I believe that God plans on using me in many other ways I can't anticipate. I'm looking forward to finding out what they are.

My prayer for you is that you find your way through these cities, fully discovering all God intends for you to learn there. I pray that you will cherish each stop along the way as a place specifically designated for your development. Reaching the fullness of your God-given purpose is the most important thing you can do in your life, and it begins right where you are.

DISCUSSION
QUESTIONS
for individual reflection or group study

INTRODUCTION

What thoughts came to mind as you read the words *chosen, holy,* and *royal* in 1 Peter 2:9? How do these words apply to *you?*

Do you believe God desires to equip each of us to be a servant-leader? Why or why not?

As you reflect on your life so far, which events have influenced you the most in developing your character, and what excites you about this opportunity to discover and fulfill what God has in store for you through your divine life purpose?

How might our lives be different if we accept Hill's invitation to discover and fulfill our divine purpose?

In what ways might knowing the realm in which God desires us to rule (serve) aid us in recognizing what God has already taught us, the value of what we are currently experiencing, and how God is equipping us for what's to come?

Chapter 1: Bethlehem, the City of Beginnings

Why is it important for each of us to face the "Where did I come from?" and "Where am I going?" questions? What kinds of things hinder us from doing this and thereby from pursuing a life of purpose?

In what ways has your childhood—and the various twists and turns of your life—affected your view of your future? How have they affected your willingness to allow God to push you to imagine a world filled with opportunities outside of your own understanding rather than focusing on your limitations?

What do you think Hill meant by this statement: "Many people die having never lived"? In light of this, no matter how insignificant we may feel, how might we begin to realize that God has a great plan for where we will go and what He will accomplish through us?

When we experience, as David did, emotional pain and rejection, we may feel forgotten and undervalued. What have been your experiences with the broken and hurt places in your heart, and what have you discovered about yourself and God in the process?

What have you learned about yourself when you've faced overwhelming odds and haven't realized that a great good and greater life were coming?

CHAPTER 2: GIBEAH, THE CITY OF EXPOSURE

For what reasons might God place us in situations that do not seem to make sense for accomplishing our calling? How might our realization that God truly desires to develop and prepare us to step into our divine purpose influence our response to these situations?

Who in your life has demonstrated that the seemingly impossible is possible? That God can and will use people from even the most troubled or insignificant families for His greater purposes? That your God-provided exposure to people is a sign that your potential exceeds your initial expectations?

Which situations have challenged you to realize that God has a greater purpose for you and that observing other people's words and actions, as David did, is an important part of learning what not to do? What situations have helped you discover your royalty and inspired you to live it out through service to God and people?

Why, as Hill pointed out, is exposure to previews of our destinies often "wrapped up in service" to others? Just as he learned that God often uses "imperfect-looking openings" to provide advancement in our lives, what practical lessons have you learned through serving other people?

What preparatory lessons might God have for you to learn right now through even brief exposure to people's positive and negative examples? How do your personal choices make a difference in whether or not you learn what to do or not do as you discover your true calling?

Hill invites us to thank God for people who equip us to learn more about leadership, even if our exposure to such people is brief. How might thankfulness for people such as Mr. Nash encourage us to face the future more confidently, believing we can make a positive difference in our families, communities, and even countries?

CHAPTER 3: VALLEY OF ELAH, THE CITY OF TRANSITION

What is the arrow principle? Why are so-called backward, tension-filled moves involving service to others not necessarily negative?

As Hill experienced often, facing our most terrifying and intimidating doors can turn out to be doorways to great blessings and amazing opportunities. Why is this? What kinds of rewards will come when we break the hold that our fears—or people around us—have on us?

Hill has concluded that the best approach to facing fearful problems is exercising one's faith through a faith-building talk with the Most High God—listening to what God says and doing it. In your estimation, how effective is this strategy, and how can a person stop listening to the giant as David did and live out the truth of Philippians 1:6 on the battlefield of faith?

What can David teach us about having a faith-filled mind-set toward "giant" challenges? How can we demonstrate a "when-I-win" mind-set grounded in God and His promises and thus confidently fight our giants on our own terms using talents God has provided?

What benefit might you (and others around you) receive from allowing biblical characters to speak into your life as Hill did? Developing a personal relationship with God and fully embracing His love? Using the talents God has already equipped you with and victories you've experienced in other areas to aid you in present struggles?

What risks are you willing to take, relying on God's power and protection, in order to move forward in transition to fulfill your purpose, even if you face criticism from friends and coworkers? (Hint: Remember, David picked up five smooth stones, not just one, as he prepared his trustworthy weapon for the task.)

CHAPTER 4: JEBUS, THE CITY OF PERSONAL PROMISE

What new or different battles are you facing (including threatening voices from your past) that require you to develop spiritually, to mature in your faith, and to set deliberate goals? Which of the spiritual weapons Hill mentioned—prayer, Bible, worship, friendship—will be most helpful in your warfare, and what others might you add to this list?

Do you agree or disagree with this statement: "The greater the level of need I bring to the Scriptures, the greater my capacity to receive more from them"? Why or why not?

Which aspects of Hill's story of painful trauma resonated with you? Why, after facing and exacming such enemy "giants" as debt and depression, should we then demonstrate to others in the body of Christ that these giants are not all-powerful?

When David took Goliath's head to Jerusalem, what was he proclaiming to himself and others? What might we learn from this about our dreams for the future and how to discern God's will for our lives?

What pain, challenges, and disappointments have stolen part or all of your ability to believe in your dreams (be honest), and what practical steps can you take today to express more faith in God, learn to discern His will for your life, and, in Hill's words, bury the heads of defeated giants in the soil of your future?

Chapter 5: Return to Gibeah, the City of Re-Equipping

How willing are you to re-equip—to learn new skills, abilities, and "weapons" in preparation for entering new cities as David did?

Why does Hill believe that prayer—the arrows of power—and the Word of God—the sword—are essential as we reassess where we are and what lies ahead? How have difficulties you have faced affected your trust in God—His love, comfort, faithfulness, protection—and thus crystallized your character and faith in Him?

As revealed in Hill's "bloody word" of personal testimony, how does God use such testimony of life change to bring down evil strongholds in people's lives and to help equip them to face their personal battles effectively?

What has been your personal experience with deeper relationships? What challenges have they presented? Why can people who truly love us with authentic, godly love influence us so much, in contrast to people whose love is purchased, prompted, or prodded?

What gives you hope as you examine the covenantal relation-ship between David and Jonathan? How can you cultivate new relationships that stretch and challenge you without dragging past pain into your present?

In light of Saul, what warnings and insights did Hill provide concerning how people we have willingly served may respond when God promotes us publicly to use gifts in new areas of influence? Concerning times when things end strangely and cause us to believe we are at our end? Concerning why we might, as David did, have to figuratively sneak out a window in order to survive?

CHAPTER 6: GATH, THE CITY IN HELL'S BACKYARD

When life experiences have put you in a discouraging tailspin, how have you approached God, and what conclusions have you reached about why He has allowed hard times to enter your life?

Just as David regrouped in Gath and prepared for his next steps, we too need such regroup times. How might our perspective change if we, as Hill wrote, view our trouble as a "promotion" and thank God for His amazing grace that gets us through?

Respond to this statement: "At times, our self-doubt blinds us and we need the outside perspective of our enemies to help us know we are progressing." How might this lead us to praise and gladness, not sadness?

Although David went to Gath without asking God first, God still used this seeming "mistake" to help David find his purpose. What do you think David learned about the limits of acting alone against an evil kingdom, and how might this have aided him later as Israel's king?

How easy is it, in today's culture, for us to maintain our identity while downplaying (hiding) our abilities in a "Gath" situation where we face an adversary we are not yet ready to confront? What implications does this kind of experience have for our choice of words, for patience, for dependence on God while we "live in Gath"?

As Hill pointed out, we cannot know God's ultimate plan for the "Sauls" in our lives who create great hardship. In light of this, why might it be better to extend mercy to such people?

CHAPTER 7: ADULLAM, THE CITY OF LEADERSHIP DEVELOPMENT

Hill has weighed the experiences of seeing the life he constructed fall apart while God put things back together in new ways that promoted His higher and perfect will. In your estimation, is the possibility of seeing God shipwreck your plans worth the price? Why or why not?

When God has used painful difficulties to shape you into who He intends for you to be, what benefits have resulted from your suffering? How can the difficulty of your situations transform you from a broken person into a God-transformed person who discovers how resilient and strong you really are?

Hill showed that God increased David's responsibilities yet did not give him all of them right away. In what ways has God's shaping of your life—including distress, debt, and discontentment—affected not only you also but others who need God's guidance in order to find a new start and who are drawn to find shelter, encouragement, and instruction through you?

What nagging questions have you had to face as a result of God's "carving process" in your life, and what may be keeping you in a place of loss, stagnation, or powerlessness rather than pursuing opportunities that promise positive change and hope?

Which people have rallied to help you faithfully during difficult situations, and how have you benefited from these special people God used to encourage your growth, even in seemingly mundane situations?

In what ways has your faith in God been "battle tested," and how have these battles shaped you, your direction in life, and your ability to thank God when you are stretched well past your imagined breaking point?

As you discover and live out the divine call on your life, pursuing your destiny in order to do something specific and important, how are your family members and friends responding?

CHAPTER 8: KEILAH, THE CITY OF BETRAYAL

Hill wrote, "The next vital lesson any person who seeks to reach their fullest potential must learn: how to survive betrayal." Based on your experiences, do you agree or disagree? Which insights into the benefits of betrayal—including important choices you can make in order to grow through betrayal—surprised you? Why?

Why do you think Hill said in this chapter that gates and walls we think will protect us can actually keep us from being free and from receiving love? Why do we have to leave them in order to grow personally, serve and lead in our communities, and show the love of Jesus in our spiritually dark world?

How does helping others, even those who witness our successes and then betray us, help us discover how strong we can become?

What insights can we gain from the betrayal Jesus willingly experienced and the spoils He received: defeating the Evil One and rescuing humanity from the bondage of sin?

Faced with betrayal, why is it sometimes best to quietly exit our Keilah so, as Hill put it, we can "live to love, trust, fight, learn, and lead another day"?

What unexpected spoils have you gained through betrayal, and in what ways is the overall perspective on betrayal in this chapter different from the way many betrayed people think and respond?

CHAPTER 9: EN GEDI, THE CITY OF REVENGE

When you have no clear acceptable options yet must choose one, how have you dealt with indecision and fear? Why doesn't God's perfect situation for you always look perfect?

Which persons have you had trouble forgiving? Why? How might you benefit by doing the hard work of extending grace to people you think don't deserve it?

How might Jesus's sacrifice on the cross and the powerful example of forgiveness He demonstrated throughout His life inform our choices to keep forgiving rather than fanning the flame of unforgiveness?

Instead of choosing revenge, rage, and toxic unforgiveness, how do we douse the fire of unforgiveness with the water of grace? What does this kind of choice require of us, including its impact on our memories of hurt and pain?

Do you believe that forgiveness is an ongoing process, not a one-time event? Why or why not?

In light of Hill's thoughts on rewriting endings, which ending(s) might you like to rewrite in order to finally be free, at peace, and not only forgiving but loving?

CHAPTER 10: ZIKLAG, THE CITY OF DISCOURAGEMENT

When and how have past disappointments in relationships with people you loved—truly terrible Ziklag situations—affected you, and how well did you deal with your wounded heart? These days, how willing are you to allow God to change your losses into wins and to teach you more about faith, decision-making, and other areas for growth?

What encouragement did you receive from this chapter?

Why is it important for us, during times of disappointment, to examine our lives, willingly seek God's guidance and freedom, and recognize how our disappointment with people can negatively affect our ability to trust God?

Hill wrote, "When you realize you have nothing left but God, you cannot help but become encouraged if you really know who God is." Do you agree or disagree? Why?

When disappointments come, do you tend to fasten yourself to the Lord, or do you try to pursue your own directions and handle things your own way?

CHAPTER 11: HEBRON, THE CITY OF ALMOST THERE

When David's long-term struggles with Saul ended, he experienced a new sense of peace and freedom. How has God used "the death of Saul" to signal that you have reached Hebron—having your divine purpose before you and heading toward the fulfillment of God's promise in your life? In what way(s) did your "Saul" help you reach this point?

Why is it important to not just look ahead to your divine purpose and destiny but to reflect on the experience, wisdom, character skills, principles, and resolve you've garnered along the way and the final lessons you are learning in order to move into your divine assignment?

Hill wrote, "The miracle of walking into your divine purpose will always be accomplished within the context of relationships." Why are key connections with the right people—those who understand who we are now and who we are to be—vital to us in fulfilling our divine destiny, and how do they enable each of us to walk into our divine purpose quite differently than those who pursue and celebrate the rugged individualism so prevalent in our world today?

When you are in Hebron, why will God likely entrust a still-familiar portion of future responsibility to you at first? Slow and arduous as this may seem, why is such a small beginning a vital part of your divine purpose?

After the pain, rejection, and dejection you've endured on the way to your goal, why should you allow God to "detox," restore, and heal you so you don't bring a "damaged you" into a prepared promise?

What may happen if you rush through the place of "almost there" and do not value this time to keep learning and celebrating each step of your journey?

As you pondered the meanings of David's wives' names, which provided you with insights into what God desires and promises to add to each of our lives as we prepare to fulfill our calling? Which meaning(s) stood out to you? Why?

CHAPTER 12: JERUSALEM, THE CITY OF DREAMS

How will you know when it's time to walk from Hebron into Jerusalem, and why are the cautions and encouragements Hill mentioned essential to your divine destiny?

Upon reflecting on your life and the various cities described in this book, what excites you as you begin to live out your God-given purpose? Why is faith still vital as you complete new assignments, allowing God's dreams for you to unfold?

Strange as it may seem, how might writing thank-you letters to people, situations, and past problems that enabled you to enter

Jerusalem not only strengthen you but also lead to praising and thanking God for all He has done and is doing in your life?

In what ways will God use even the most painful aspects of your life to not only fulfill your destiny but also draw people to Him who also need spiritual healing?

In light of this, why does God often challenge us to get "dirty, stinky, and slimy" in order to fulfill His divine purposes, and how does He change our pain into power as we apply biblical truths to our lives?

Hill wrote, "We can experience our tomorrows only if we walk out of our yesterdays." How does remembering the following points aid us in our Jerusalem as the promise of our destiny unfolds: who we are; what God has brought us through; why our active faith can overcome our negative circumstances; and God's continued presence in our lives?

Why, in many respects, will our journey of reaching the fullness of our God-given purpose never end while we are still on this earth?